THE PROTESTANT FACE
OF ANGLICANISM

The Protestant Face
of Anglicanism

PAUL F. M. ZAHL

WILLIAM B. EERDMANS PUBLISHING COMPANY
GRAND RAPIDS, MICHIGAN / CAMBRIDGE, U.K.

© 1998 Wm. B. Eerdmans Publishing Co.
255 Jefferson Ave. S.E., Grand Rapids, Michigan 49503 /
P.O. Box 163, Cambridge CB3 9PU U.K.

Printed in the United States of America

02 01 00 99 98   7 6 5 4 3 2 1

Zahl, Paul F. M.
The Protestant face of Anglicanism / Paul F. M. Zahl.
p.   cm.
Includes bibliographical references.
ISBN 0-8028-3775-1 (alk. paper)
1. Anglican Communion — History. 2. Church of England — History.
3. Episcopal Church — History. 4. Protestantism. I. Title.
BX5005.Z34   1998
283 — dc21   97-38522
CIP

*This book is dedicated to the parish family of
the Cathedral Church of the Advent
Birmingham, Alabama*

Contents

Introduction

In September 1896 the Archbishop of Canterbury, Edward White Benson, paid an official visit to Ireland. The first public meeting he attended was held in Dublin; its purpose was to aid the restoration of Kildare Cathedral. At the meeting Benson saw opposite the platform a motto that described the Church of Ireland as "Catholic, Apostolic, Reformed, and Protestant," and he took the occasion to say that the English had not been careful enough to teach the "mass of our people" the history of the Church of England. He said, "You cannot justify those four words, 'Catholic,' 'Apostolic,' 'Reformed' and 'Protestant,' unless you teach everybody you have to do with 'why you are what you are.'"

On October 9, two days before his death, the archbishop returned to one of those four words.

> If ever it was necessary, if ever we began to doubt whether it was necessary, to lay so much emphasis upon that last word [the word "Protestant"], I think that events of the last few weeks, and the tone which has been adopted towards this primeval Church of Ireland and England, are things which warn us that that word is not to be forgotten.

Benson was referring to the pope's encyclical declaring Anglican ordination to be "absolutely null and utterly void." He added:

1

It is not a word to be forgetting; but it is a word to be understood — a word which must not be used as a secular war-cry. Those are words which have a deep meaning for our children, which we should try to penetrate, and which we should hand down to them to be cherished for ever.[1]

The *theme* of this book is the concept *Protestant* in relation to Anglicanism. More broadly, the theme of the book is the concept *Protestant* in its relation to Christianity as a whole, and, even more broadly, its relation to the world that surrounds the Christian Church. If this concept still has meaning for the specifically Anglican expression of Christianity, then it should also bear application to the whole of Christianity. What if *Protestant*, moreover, were a concept linking the ancient claims of Christianity with specific contemporary hurts and yearnings? That is the vista which this book seeks to open.

The *purpose* of the book is first to restore the image within the Anglican tradition, indeed within the larger Christian Church, of the Protestant legacy of faith. Our hope is to bring to light again a view of Christianity that has been cherished by millions of people in the past and still has something to contribute to the greater Christian movement in the world. This view of Christianity is called Protestant Anglicanism.

The second purpose of the book is to demonstrate the present potential contribution of this view of Christianity to a world that exists in conscious search of enduring foundations and orientation. There is a resource here which needs to be better known.

From its beginning as a distinct category of Christianity, Anglicanism has shown two different faces. It has from the time of the English Reformation been a Janus. One face, recalling Archbishop Benson's four words, has been "Catholic" and "Apostolic," while the other face has been "Reformed" and "Protestant." The relative prominence or visibility of each face has varied from period to period,

1. *Archbishop Benson in Ireland: A Record of His Irish Sermons and Addresses* (London, 1896), pp. 26, 27, 110, 111, as quoted in Henry Edmund Wace, *Principles of the Reformation: Practical and Historical Questions* (London, 1910), pp. 1-3.

sometimes from epoch to epoch, in the history of the Church. We could say that the face of Anglicanism in the eighteenth century was almost completely the Reformed and Protestant one. We could say that the face of Anglicanism in the last quarter of the nineteenth century and the first half of the twentieth was almost completely the Catholic and Apostolic one.

A third profile came into view after 1860, the year in which the controversial progressivist book *Essays and Reviews* was published. This is the "liberal" face of Anglicanism. At times this third face has taken on Protestant shadings, at times Catholic ones. There have been "liberal Evangelicals" and there have been "liberal Catholics." But the core expression of Anglicanism is not a trinity of persons but rather a Janus. It presents either a "Catholic" or a "Protestant" face. This fact stems from our history. It stems, as much as from any one source, from the religious ambivalence of Queen Elizabeth I, whose reign embodied the tensions within the Church she "settled." This ambivalence of two traditions, the Catholic and the Protestant, has been with us ever since. It shows no sign of abating.

The historic tension between the two traditions, Catholic and Protestant, that struggle for the Anglican Church's soul has more recently been resolved by a school of thought which favors the view that Anglicanism is a *balance* rather than a tension, a *synthesis* rather than an antithesis, a *tertium quid* or "third way" rather than an either/or. This view tends to reduce the vital claims inherent to both distinct presentations of Christianity to a sort of combination of ideas: "reformed Catholicism" or "catholic Evangelicalism" or the like. This view draws down the distinctive strengths of the two competing traditions to the claim of a harmonious mix, one tradition broadening out or augmenting the other to create a separate and distinct entity, "Anglicanism."

Thus there are now two fundamental ways of describing the Janus profile of Anglicanism. Either it is a tension between two contrasting views of Christianity, one Catholic and one Protestant; or it is a union of opposites, as in Zen Buddhism, producing a *third* distinct entity, the elusive *tertium quid*. How could we describe this third entity? It is spoken of as moderation in all things; the virtue of

Englishness, by which is meant an unsystematic, unaxiomatic approach to truth and a certain disposition to quietness and reserve over against affirmation and statement; and a deliberate ambiguity that reflects the world as it really is. This view of the thing as third entity is put forward with conviction by John Booty in his entry on "Anglicanism" in the 1996 *Oxford Encyclopedia of the Reformation*.

But there is an important flaw in this way of viewing Anglicanism as the union of opposites resulting in a third, more valid way. It tends to elevate aspects of Christianity that are of secondary importance in responding to the problem of being human. The aspects of Christianity that are of primary importance in addressing the problem of being human are themes such as "redemption and release" (Hymn 539, *The Hymnal 1982*), atonement and grace, freedom versus bondage, and the question, Who is Jesus Christ? On the view of Anglicanism as a third way of seeing Christianity, these core themes subside to a lesser position of interest. The passion and energy, according to the "third-way" school of thought, relate to Anglican "distinctives" concerning worship and liturgy; so-called sacred time, sacred space, and sacred rhythm; "decency" and "orderliness"; and complicated arguments concerning the sources of religious authority. The Anglican "distinctives" of the third way prove to be tepid and fairly low-octane appeals on the relative scale of response to the furious calls from the world for an antidote to its pain. The third way sells short what we have to offer.

Dean E. A. Litton, in his massive 1882/1892 *Introduction to Dogmatic Theology*, one of the few attempts in the history of the Church of England to compose a systematic Christian theology, argued against the "Anglicanism as third entity" proposal. He wrote, in high-flying prose typical of the period,

> It has been a matter of debate whether or not the Anglican Church is a Protestant Church, and whether or not she possesses a theology of her own, neither that of Rome nor yet of Geneva, but occupying a mid-way position between the two. . . . Whatever might be the character of the Anglican Church as a whole, the Thirty-Nine Articles, at any rate, admit of no doubt

4

as to their parentage; at least as regards those points on which they differ from the Church of Rome. . . . The Anglican Church, if she is to be judged by the statements of the Articles, must be ranked amongst the Protestant Churches of Europe. (xi)

Romanism (including its mutilated counterpart, Anglo-Catholicism) is a religion of the incarnation, the virtue of which is communicated by sacraments; Protestantism is a religion of the atonement, the virtue of which is appropriated by direct faith in Christ, His word and His work, not, however, to the exclusion of sacraments in their proper place. . . . On neither side are these cordial facts of revelation, or their connexion, denied; there could have been no atonement if there had not been an incarnation; but the stress laid on the one or the other, and particularly differences of view as regards the instrument of appropriation, may affect our whole conception of Christianity and lead to widely divergent theological systems. (xiv)

Independently of the difficulties attending an attempt to establish a special Anglican theology . . . the writer must avow his conviction that, in a scientific point of view, *all such attempts will probably end in failure;* and that there are only two systems of Dogmatic Theology, the Romish and the Protestant. (xii; italics added)[2]

The underlying premise for this study of the Protestant face of Anglicanism is an understanding that Anglicanism is a tension between two divergent schools of thought within Christianity. Anglicanism is an umbrella that stretches, for reasons relating primarily to the history and politics of Tudor, Jacobean, and Stuart England, over two different and perhaps ultimately irreconcilable presentations of the religion of Jesus. This means that the history of the Church,

2. E. A. Litton, *Introduction to Dogmatic Theology,* ed. Philip E. Hughes (1882, 1892; London, 1960).

Litton became dean of Oriel College, Oxford, in 1843 and wrote his book while he was rector of Naunton, near Cheltenham.

5

both in England and among the daughter churches outside England, has been a changeable face, depending on the ascendancy, at any given period, of one school of thought over the other. It is as if the Janus face of the Church is seldom revealed to us in full. Rather the light of a specific age and time, with its specific concerns, shines more directly on one or the other of its profiles.

Although this study attempts to shine the light more directly on the Protestant profile of the Church, it is not an exercise in anti-Catholicism. Others have illuminated the distinctly Catholic insights and trends within historic Anglicanism. The point here is to burnish one profile, the Protestant profile, which appears tarnished and neglected today, rusted and even in pieces. This is a positive statement concerning one undeniably important perspective on the whole.

Who would deny that the Protestant face of Anglicanism is not highlighted in the present day? Who would deny that the Catholic face of Anglicanism is also not highlighted at present, although it was, in its "liberal Catholic" phase, ascendant in most sectors until *Honest to God*[3] and the 1960s? Today it is safe to say that the "Anglicanism as third entity" view prevails or at least engages the attention of most who would identify and define Anglicanism. A visit to the "Anglicanism" section of any church or seminary bookstore confirms this. Anglicanism is a wax nose. It can be seen as the ultimate balanced *Western* form of Eastern Orthodoxy or as the best haven for seekers after a spirituality of the hallowing of all created things within the sacramental principle (whatever exactly that is).[4]

But Anglicanism is not a wax nose! Or better, it will not serve

---

3. This book was published in 1962 by Bishop John A. T. Robinson. At the time it seemed to "blow the lid off" the Church of England, with its frank admissions of doubt and skepticism, much of them refashioned from the German theologians Rudolf Bultmann and Paul Tillich.

4. Thus A. M. Allchin's catchall definition: "The salient features of the Anglican spiritual tradition over the last four centuries (are) in particular its search for wholeness and balance, its desire at once to spread itself outwards in a concern for all human life, and at the same time to turn inwards, to explore the heights and depths of the mystery of God's presence at the heart of human life" ("Anglican Spirituality," in *The Study of Anglicanism*, ed. Stephen Sykes and John Booty [London and Minneapolis, 1988], p. 322).

the world if it becomes one. The face will lose its profile. The salt will lose its savor. Better to see it as a jostling, jammed, glass telephone booth filled with strangers, constrained by geography to remain in some relation. The cry of at least one of those strangers will be heard above the din.

This writer seeks to restore the distinctly Protestant face of Anglicanism. What has it meant in the past to see oneself as a Protestant Anglican? Where has the good news been in that? What contribution does the Protestant ethos within Anglicanism have to make? And not only to this Communion, but to the whole field of Christianity upon a pluralistic earth?

Even if they are somewhat narrowly construed, in the spirit of his time, do Bishop J. C. Ryle's words of February 1, 1900, have something positive to say to us today?

> Cling to the old Church of England — cling to its Bible, its Prayer Book and its Articles. . . . Never forget that the principles of the Protestant Reformation made this country what she is, and let nothing ever tempt you to forsake them.[5]

Bishop Ryle rarely failed to use the words "Reformed," "Protestant," and "Evangelical" in connection with the Church of England. An Anglicanism distinct from these three qualifiers did not exist for him.

In words more broadly construed, what contribution could the quality of Anglicanism described here by Michael Saward offer to the enterprise of Christian mission in the modern world?

> The Anglican establishment often looks at itself and sees itself midway between Catholic and Evangelical extremes. But that depends upon one's point of viewing. Suppose you were to take the full perspective of worldwide Christianity? Suddenly all looks different. Consider the continuum. Right in the centre stands

---

5. Ryle's final Episcopal address, as reprinted in J. C. Ryle, *Charges and Addresses* (Edinburgh and Carlisle, 1978), p. 368.

the Anglican Evangelical. He has retained the major essentials of historic Catholic and Orthodox Christianity — creeds, episcopacy, three-fold ministry, sacramental liturgy. But there is another side to him. He, like all the Christians who look back to the Reformation with gratitude, uses his Bible as a sure guide. He knows what it is to seek for, and usually to experience, a personal conversion. He cannot rest content with the outward signs of Catholicity — he looks for a felt spiritual experience within a shared "priesthood of all believers." The Anglican Evangelical has, in short, discovered himself at the pivotal point of worldwide Christianity. . . . If he has eyes to see this he does not feel ashamed. He sees the virtues of a blend of continuity and spontaneity, of objectivity and subjectivity.[6]

The Protestant Anglican, displaying the Protestant face of Anglicanism: Is there something here for us at a time of considerable unease in the Communion? Is there something on offer here, a facet to be repolished, a legacy to be rediscovered, a profile to be restored? I believe there is.

6. Michael Saward, *Evangelicals on the Move* (London, 1987), pp. 91-92.

CHAPTER 1

The English Reformation: Detour or Defining Moment

"The human mind is always urgent for action, impatient of obstacles, and eager for liberty and conclusions; it willingly forgets facts which impede and cramp it; but in forgetting, it does not destroy them; they subsist to condemn it someday and convict it of error."

FRANÇOIS GUIZOT

The battle for the identity and interpretation of the Protestant Reformation in England began even while the events that shaped it were taking place. Who were the victims and who were the persecutors? Who were the heroes and who the villains? How should we compare the reports concerning Protestant martyrs under Queen Mary and Catholic martyrs under Queen Elizabeth? A lot depends on one's point of view.

Standing in a field near Sandford-on-Thames with a dedicated vicar of liberal Catholic sympathy, I heard him describe the martyrdom of a priest who was burned close to a barn within sight of us. It took me five minutes to realize that the sufferer had been Roman Catholic. "Martyr?!" I thought. "How about traitor!" It was a thought I kept to myself, for that priest killed under Queen Elizabeth had shown as much human courage as my own icons Latimer and Ridley had twenty years earlier.

Almost five centuries of competition over the "ownership" of the Reformation legacy in England has not seen the issue resolved.[1] There are Catholic views and there are Protestant views, even down to the weight placed on county record-office statistics. Today we would probably see A. G. Dickens[2] and Patrick Collinson[3] as Protestant interpreters, if only in the way they understand the evidence. We would certainly see Christopher Haigh[4] as a Catholic interpreter.

Another area of contention is the question of whether the English Reformation was really over *religion* at all. Was it at root a national change in theology, or was it, rather, an economic upheaval, stimulated from the designs of an aspiring *nouveaux* upper class on monastic and other church property, especially land? This is called the laicizing of landed capital! Or was the English Reformation simply the expression of changing fortunes on the part of king-maker nobles, like Somerset, Northumberland, and Norfolk, not to mention the rivalry of the children of Henry VIII? Or was it the attempt of a small minority of religious "radicals" (i.e., the Protestant intellectuals) to impose their ideas on the larger majority of conservative Englishmen (i.e., the Catholic "people")? Was it a justified attack launched merely upon late medieval abuses and lapses of discipline within the Church? What was the real *subject* of the English Reformation?

On this topic A. G. Dickens's summary has probably never been bettered:

1. See Rosemary O'Day, *The Debate on the English Reformation* (Oxford, London, and New York, 1982).

2. See A. G. Dickens, *The English Reformation*, 2d ed. (London, 1989).

3. See, for example, Patrick Collinson, *The Religion of Protestants: The Church in English Society 1559-1625*, Ford Lectures 1979 (Oxford, 1982).

4. See, for example, Christopher Haigh, *Reformation and Resistance in Tudor Lancashire* (Cambridge, 1975).

In the forgoing account we have sought to understand the English Reformation as an integral part of the European Reformation, and also to see the whole movement as more profound, more radical than any mere attack upon the disciplinary shortcomings of the late medieval Church. . . . We have observed conflicts between King and Pope, Church and State, common lawyers and canon lawyers, laymen and clerics, ecclesiastical and lay landowners, citizens and bishops. We have witnessed many ideological clashes on church government and finance, clerical privilege, Church-State relations, the rôle of ecclesiastical law, the definition of heresy. The theologies of the eucharist, justification and grace. *But above all we have learned to view the movement as most essentially a process of Protestantization among the English people,* a process not always favoured by the State, a process exerting a mass of direct and indirect influences not only upon English history but upon much of western civilization. For the present writer *the unifying theme lies in a change of viewpoint concerning the documents, nature and functions of religion,* both in the individual and in society.[5]

Dickens's mature view of the Reformation crisis is one that does justice to that crisis as a change in *religion.* It is this essential change from the religion of Catholics to the "religion of Protestants" (William Chillingworth's phrase from 1638) which is the subject of the English Reformation. It is a change which has been effaced in profile and in general understanding. It is a change which makes up the base contours of the Protestant profile of Anglicanism.

What change in religious viewpoint was achieved by the English Reformation?

5. Dickens, *The English Reformation,* pp. 380-81.

Period I: The Reign of Henry VIII (1509-1547)

Soon after Luther posted the Ninety-Five Theses at Wittenberg on the Eve of All Saints', October 31, 1517, his ideas concerning forgiveness and justification before God, the bound human will, and the free grace of God spread to England. A circle of Cambridge University teachers began to study Luther's ideas. Several were converted to the "new religion," as it began to be called. England's earliest Protestant Reformers included Thomas Bilney, who was probably the first Protestant and Evangelical in the history of the English Church; John Frith; and Robert Barnes. Quickly they were followed by Thomas Cranmer, Nicholas Ridley, Hugh Latimer, and, as important as any of them, William Tyndale. John Foxe also requires special mention, as he became the chronicler of the Reformation, fully contemporary with the events of Protestantism's changing fortunes. Initially, and ultimately in almost every case, these men were risking their lives.

In embracing Protestantism as a recovered orthodoxy, recovered, that is, from the Bible, they began to understand the "old religion" as heresy. At the same moment, they were judged as heretics by the Church in whose holy orders they had spent their adult lives. Although persecution came in waves, with pauses even of years in between, England's earliest Protestants were marked men. This was true right through to the break with Rome in 1529 on account of the King's "great matter," Henry's divorce.

What caused these scholars, for humanist scholars they were, to risk everything for the Protestant faith? It was in the first place a *positive* and, for them, wholly *new* insight. Rather than a protest in the initial situation, what changed their course was an affirmation. This affirmation was the doctrine of justification by faith, or more properly, justification by grace through faith. It concerned the way God deals with men and women, his creatures. The doctrine is summed up well by William Tyndale in his 1527 commentary on St. Luke 16:1-9. It is entitled *The Parable of the Wicked Mammon*, and is the *locus classicus* of early English Protestant belief:

A good tree bringeth forth good fruit, and a bad tree bringeth forth bad fruit. There seest thou that the fruit makes not the tree good, but the tree the fruit; and that the tree must be good, or made good, before it can bring forth good fruit. . . . So is this true and nothing more true — that a man before all good works must first be good, and that it is impossible that works should make him good, if he were not good before he did good works. . . . This is therefore a plain, and a sure conclusion not to be doubted of, that there must be first in the heart of a man before he do any good works, a greater and a more precious thing than all the good works in the world, to reconcile him to God, to bring the love and favour of God to him, to make him love God again, to make him righteous and good in the sight of God, to do away his sin, to deliver him and loose him out of that captivity wherein he was conceived and born, in which he could neither love God, nor the will of God. Or else how can he work any good work that should please God, if there were not some supernatural goodness in him, given of God freely, whereof that good work must spring? even as a sick man must first be healed or made whole, ere he can do the deeds of a whole man; and as the blind man must first have sight given him, ere he can see; and he that hath his feet in fetters, gyves, or stocks, must first be loosed, ere he can go, walk, or run. . . .

This precious thing which must be in the heart, before a man can work any good work, is the word of God, which in the gospel preacher, proffers, and brings unto all that repent and believe, the favour of God in Christ. Whosoever hears the word and believes it, the same is thereby righteous, and thereby is given him the Spirit of God, which leads him unto all that is the will of God, and he is loosed from the captivity and bondage of the devil, and his heart is free to love God, and desires to do the will of God. Therefore it is called the word of life, the word of grace, the word of health, the word of redemption, the word of forgiveness, and the word of peace.[6]

6. *The Parable of the Wicked Mammon*, from *Writings of the Rev. William Tyndale* (Lewes, Sussex, 1986 reprint), pp. 19-20.

William Tyndale is quoted at some length because he presents the clarity and focus of the early English Reformers. They understood from Luther, who had redirected them from scholastic theology to the Scriptures, that the human condition exists in a boundness analogous to a man who is sick. This man cannot choose the good. The very law of God afflicts him more, because it commands him to do what he cannot by his own efforts do. In the good news of the forgiveness of sin through Christ, however, a new being comes to birth within the inwardness of the self. A new confidence of belovedness, rooted in pardon, breaks in upon the bound being. This pardon is sufficient to break the chains and cause a new heart to grow. This new heart wishes to do the good spontaneously, and no longer under compulsion, under protest, or at best half-heartedly. The new being, righteous by the verdict of God, is able to act freely. The new heart, in short, is freed to love.

For Tyndale and his Protestant contemporaries, the problem of being human existed *in nuce* within the following dilemma: How can I do what my conscience tells me to do, as opposed to not doing so, or even doing the opposite of what my conscience tells me to do? The "old religion," as expressed in what we now call "late medieval scholastic theology," had in not one of its expressions conveyed the dramatic *release* that justification by grace through faith, now so passionately expressed by Tyndale above, was able to do. The human being needed justification before that authority which is ultimate: God. All efforts to achieve that justification, or recognition, or legitimization, or even "inclusion," as late twentieth-century parlance might put it, were seen to be failures. The unfree character of human choices and aspirations was unveiled before the Reformers with a penetration almost unique in the history of thought.[7] The justifying *grace*, or unmerited favor of God in Christ, now really meant something. It shifted the burden of human legitimization from the self to God, specifically to God's forgiveness of sin. Were this grace just embraced, trusted, *held* by faith (i.e., assented to from the heart),

7. See Hannah Arendt, "The Apostle Paul and the Impotence of the Will," in *The Life of the Mind*, vol. 2 (New York, 1977), pp. 63-73.

everything could change. The sun would rise, the fog would break, and freedom could begin.

That was the heart and soul of early English Protestantism. It would later become a given, a conviction referred to as basic and fundamental. It would remain the signature of Anglican Protestantism, right up to the present moment. In its earliest inbreaking — and Tyndale's piece remains the touchstone — it was a thunderbolt. Hugh Latimer reported later that when he heard it, meaning justification by faith, for the first time, from Thomas Bilney, the hair on his head stood on end.

The reign of Henry VIII was, right up to the very end, an uncertain period for Protestantism in England. Henry's "even-handedness" in matters of religion meant that he executed roughly the same number of Catholics (i.e., those who would not accept his authority in deposing the pope as Supreme Head of the Church of England) as Protestants (i.e., those who challenged, mainly in the printed word, his still un-Reformed theology and the conservative articles he promulgated to stabilize the religious situation when things seemed to be veering too far to the Protestant side). The story of Henry's reign as it applied to the fluid fortunes of Protestantization in England is told densely and well in the recent biography of Thomas Cranmer by Diarmaid MacCulloch.[8]

All that needs to be added here is that the Protestant face of Anglicanism was in creation, though well veiled and even underground, from the early 1520s. Only at the very end did Henry tip the scales by choosing a Protestant protector for his son and successor, Edward VI. This tipping of the scales can be attributed directly to the influence of Henry's sixth wife, the Protestant Catherine Parr. Queen Catherine deserves her own chapter in any history of the Protestant face of Anglicanism, for she steered an extraordinarily wise, patient, and tactful course in a lake of sharks where the Catholic duke of Norfolk and the bishop of London sought any possible

8. Diarmaid MacCulloch, *Thomas Cranmer: A Life* (London and New Haven, 1996).

excuse to discredit her, alienate Henry from her, and see her murdered.

John Foxe's description of Henry's death provides a moving glimpse into the state of affairs at the end of Henry's reign (28 January 1547). The words before and after the quotation are Diarmaid MacCulloch's:

> By the time that Cranmer reached [Henry] in the small hours of that morning, Henry was already incapable of speech, but reached out to his old friend.
>
> "Then the archbishop, exhorting him to put his trust in Christ, and to call upon his mercy, desired him, though he could not speak, yet to give some token with his eyes or with his hand, that he trusted in the Lord. The King, holding him with his hand, did wring his hand in his as hard as he could."
>
> Quietly playing out his calling as royal chaplain, Cranmer had won a final victory in his years of argument with the King on justification. No last rites for Henry; no extreme unction; just an evangelical statement of faith in a grip of the hand.[9]

When Henry died, the veiled face of the "new church" was almost ready to be revealed. There had been glimpses in production, like the first official Bible in English (1539) and the preferment within the Church of certain men of known Protestant principles. But the formal profile still looked "Henrician Catholic." And there have been some ever since who see the Reformation as a change of form (with the monarch, rather than the bishop of Rome, as Supreme Head), and not a change of substance. But the whole trend of the story puts the balance clearly in favor of Protestantism. For our purposes, the English Reformation reached its conclusion in the Glorious Revolution of 1688. But there were many turns of the screw before that final defining moment of the greater defining moment that is the change of religion in the English-speaking Church (and churches) from Catholic to Protestant.

9. MacCulloch, p. 360.

16

Period II: The Reign of Edward VI (1547-1553)

Because Edward was only nine years old when his father died, his reign was shadow-governed by two Lord Protectors, both Protestants and both worldly courtiers. Somerset ruled until an insider coup in 1549. Northumberland ruled until Edward's death in 1553. Protestantism and power politics were intertwined during the entire reign of Edward. That was true, however, in all governments during the Reformation period. The competing claims of powerful personalities, dynasties, and other interest groups need not blind us to the observation that the underlying issue on all fronts, from the protagonists' point of view, was the issue of religion.

Because both Edward's tutors and his protectors were conscious Protestants, and because Henry had ended his reign by explicit nods to the Protestant side, the reign of Edward became a sort of high tide for the promulgation of justification by faith in England. We can put it this way because it is what the Reformers consciously thought they were doing. They were ushering in a new day for the fortunes of Christianity in England, in which the gospel would take precedence over all other factors in religion and would also become the orientation point for the whole ongoing life of the Church.

Under Edward, the Book of Common Prayer was published, first in 1549, then in altered form in 1552. Under Edward, Protestant bishops were appointed in numbers and the near-impossible task of evangelizing all England by means of the English Bible began. Under Edward, Archbishop Cranmer, as also the Universities of Oxford and Cambridge, formed important links with the Protestant Reformers in Continental Europe. There was also some considerable iconoclasm, although this has been exaggerated and was by order of Parliament and Crown, not the actions of private spite or localized fanaticism.

It is astonishing how much was accomplished in so brief a period of time, less than seven years. The progress that was now made in unveiling and then chiseling into some definite form the Protestant face of Christianity in England cannot be explained except by ref-

17

erence to the years of undercurrent and proscribed study that had already taken place under Henry.

What was achieved under the son was the fruit of preparation and circumspection under the father.

Period III: The Reign of Queen Jane (1553)

From the afternoon of July 9, 1553, to the afternoon of July 16, sixteen-year-old Lady Jane Grey was Queen of England. Fearing the accession of Henry VIII's Roman Catholic daughter, Mary, Protector Northumberland pressured King Edward, during his dying days, to sign a document naming his cousin Jane as successor to the throne. Jane was the granddaughter of Henry VIII's sister Mary. Her claim to the throne was therefore distant, and she was not in legitimate succession. Northumberland arranged her marriage to his son, Guildford Dudley, and then attempted to use her as a breakfront to the wave of Catholicism that would undoubtedly crash down upon the Reformation with Mary's accession. Northumberland's scheme failed. Mary got away in time to gather an army in East Anglia, Northumberland's army deserted him, and Queen Jane was deposed, a "nine days' wonder." She and her husband were beheaded at the Tower of London on February 12, 1554. They both died as ardent Protestants.

This very brief chapter in the dynastic struggle that was the backdrop for the Protestantization of England is important, more important than it is usually estimated to be. It is important because it concerns a woman in whom learning and the Protestant faith were combined to a remarkably articulate degree. Like Catherine Parr and the tragic martyr Anne Askew, Jane Grey displays the role of educated Protestant women in the English Reformation. So impressed were her contemporaries in Europe by Jane's standing firm for justification by faith[10] that the French poet Agrippa d'Aubigné wrote of

---

10. An account of her examination by the Catholic priest Fecknam in February 1554 has been preserved. See *The Renaissance in England*, ed. J. V. Cunningham (New York, 1966), pp. 14-18.

her with deepest admiration in his epic masterpiece *Les Tragiques* (1577-1590). Later generations, especially in the nineteenth century, would see Jane as a tragic heroine, a prisoner of conscience, a girl who was used and abused but then fell in love with her husband. What she really was is plain in the few letters and prayers that remain from her: a person for whom the "new religion" was everything, the animating fire and the hope of glory. The full story of the Reformation's female heroes has yet to be written. Justification by faith was not a gender issue.

Period IV: The Reign of Mary I (1553-1558)

Mary Tudor, known forever after as "Bloody Mary," saw her accession as God's moment to re-Catholicize England. This was the most important business of her life. She was as committed to her cause as her most devoted antagonists were to theirs. Unlike most Protestants, however, she had an untouched medieval worldview that made it intolerable that heretics should even be allowed to live. In this respect she resembled Sir Thomas More, who hated the Protestants so much that he sent spies overseas to trap them on foreign ground. William Tyndale had been assassinated because of More.

How many Protestants Mary actually ordered to be burned has never been precisely clear. As with all questions concerning the Reformation in England, there are differing estimates, some in the thousands and some as low as three hundred. Probably between four and five hundred Protestants were burned alive for heresy during her reign. Even the low estimate is an enormously high number, inconceivable even, for the English. The English had no tradition to compare with the Spanish Inquisition. Moreover, Mary had heretics burned from the highest in the land (Cranmer, Latimer, Ridley, and Hooper) to the lowest (cobblers in Essex, pregnant women in East Anglia, even some feeble-minded who could barely understand why they were being chained to the stake). Mary married King Philip I of Spain, who saw himself as the anointed hammer of the Protestants. She imported Spanish priests and friars to interrogate her subjects in the manner of the Inquisition, a manner alien to the self-understanding of the English.

The result of Mary's bloody-mindedness was the almost complete discrediting of the Catholic cause in England. By the time she died (of ovarian cancer) in 1559, the nation was hungering for the return of the "new religion." Only certain ancient families, primarily in the North, remained loyal, and cryptically so, to Rome. "Bloody Mary's" six years as queen was the turning point of the Protestant Reformation in England.

Period V: The Reign of Elizabeth I (1558-1603)

Queen Elizabeth was responsible both for the restoration of the Protestant face of the English Church *and* for the ambiguity that made later generations of English Christians susceptible to its effacement.

In the first place, she acceded as Protestant queen *by definition.* This was because, from Rome's point of view, she was illegitimate. She was the daughter of Anne Boleyn, who from the Roman vantage had not been Henry's legal wife. Her birth had been the fruit, if not the occasion, of Henry's break with Rome. Moreover, Elizabeth's mother had been an early, earnest Protestant, before whose execution Archbishop Cranmer had protested quite courageously to Henry. Third, Elizabeth was excommunicated by the pope in 1570, not really very long after her accession. She was by accident of birth, maternal sympathy, and later inevitable force of circumstance England's Protestant queen. This is not to mention the fact that Protestantism was imputed to her, whether she liked it or not, by the overwhelming majority of the English people, who greeted her coming to the throne with sincere relief. Mary had alienated almost everybody, first by her burning of the Protestants and then by her marriage to the King of Spain.

The Elizabethan Protestant movement, the national Protestant feelings of the people as they actually were, is captured by a novel for young people published by Charles Kingsley in 1855. For a rich and emotional journey into the heart of Elizabeth's reign, *Westward Ho!* has never been improved upon. Moreover, it concludes with a Christian act of forgiveness and reconciliation that carries the historical elements into the realm of universal Christian drama.[11]

Nevertheless, Elizabeth inherited from her father, as distinct from her mother, an entrenched fear of civil war. That fear went back to the Wars of the Roses, the specter of which hung over every Tudor monarch. This was because the founder of the dynasty, Henry VII, had gotten the crown by violence. Elizabeth was also, by nature, *conservative*, and she would instinctively react to pressure, which came mostly, as it turned out, from the "forward" Protestants. These, even among her courtiers, not to mention her bishops, wished to hasten the pace of reform in the Church. The queen was therefore capable of "getting her back up." She deliberately retained a crucifix in her private chapel long after she had made her point concerning the royal prerogative — almost in proportion to the heat she had received from her (uniformly) Protestant bishops. She punished Archbishop Grindal completely out of proportion to his "offense," which was to defend local clergy conferences on preaching. She sequestered him because he attempted, courageously, to lecture her.

The results of Elizabeth's anxiety over potential division in the realm *and* her stubborn streak created a somewhat uncertain climate for the later period of Reformation settlement. Even her greatly trusted Archbishop John Whitgift was delivered the curveball of his life when she vetoed his Lambeth Articles in 1595, articles of religion that had been intended to be added to the Thirty-Nine, thus making more precise one aspect of "Calvinist" teaching. The question on the minds of her bishops during most of her reign was, How Protestant is she? No one questioned her essential Reformation position, sustained by lineage and the force of history (culminating in the defeat of the Spanish Armada in 1588). But the details were left somewhat sketchy. Thus the way was open for a picture of Anglicanism that was definitely Protestant but vague on some of the fine points. Later

---

11. Charles Kingsley, *Westward Ho!* (1855; New York, 1920).

catholicizing elements in the Church would take advantage of these gaps in the design.

Period VI: The Tide Goes Out
and Comes Back In (1603-1688)

At Elizabeth's death, the Church of England was Protestant, national, and consciously allied, at all levels, with the Protestant cause in Europe. The greater Protestant cause was coming under violent attack from the Hapsburg Monarchy. In 1620 the Thirty Years War would begin, and large areas of formerly Reformed or Lutheran dominion would be reconquered by Catholic armies. Had it not been for King Gustavus Adolphus of Sweden, the Reformation might have been finished in Europe, so great was the force and violence of the Roman Catholic reaction to it.

England experienced its own form of Counter-Reformation. England came within a heartbeat — James II's heartbeat — of changing its religion *again*.

The causes of the reaction to Reformation teaching within the Church of England were intellectual, theological, and also genetic.

First, the reaction was an intellectual reaction to the double predestination teachings of the more extreme wing of the generally Calvinist Anglican establishment. "Free Will"–ism and *anti-Calvinism* were the watchwords of a small party of bishops under James I (1603-1625). This party gathered around William Laud, who would become the Archbishop of Canterbury (1625-1649) under Charles I. This group was not only repulsed by Calvinism within the Church but had a horror of republican tendencies among the Puritans, tendencies challenging the power not only of kings but also of bishops. In Laud and his party a desire to reassert prelatical episcopacy (i.e., episcopacy with political privileges) was united with an allergy to pure Protestantism. Laud's perspective took advantage of the gaps or sketchy areas within the Elizabethan Reformation settlement to reassert ideas that ran implicitly, though not always explicitly, counter to it. There was also an aesthetic

22

tinge to his thinking, which understood Protestantism as dreary and lacking in drama.

The reaction we are speaking of was theological, in that it reflected a constant, recurring flight from the doctrines of grace, a flight which has ever weakened the Christian Church. *Grace* as a doctrine is being forever greeted, in the second generation of its reception, by the anxiety that it will lead to *license*. From evidence in the letters of St. Paul, not to mention the Pharisees' worry over the attitude of Jesus to the Law of Moses, the promise of the unconditional love of God penetrates to a human fear of freedom. The logic is that if "I" am loved *in spite of* my sin, then that may remove deterrence *from* my sin. Or, classically, "Are we to sin that grace may abound?" (Rom. 6:1; 3:8; 6:15). This fear is met in Christian *practice* by the fact that love, not license, is the characteristic fruit of grace. Righteousness from love, rather than unrighteousness arising from the freedom from compunction, is the result of grace affirmed.

But the anxious voice of the law insinuates itself chronically and devilishly into the Christian movement once the grace of God is preached. In the case of the second and third generations of the English Reformers, the voice of law became loud due to the hardening, on the Reformed side, of ideas concerning grace into ideas concerning election. If God does it *all* — and I contribute nothing to my salvation — then *how* does he do it, and why? Justification by grace through faith, because it posits the *bound* condition of the human being before the advent of grace, posits the total *freedom* of God. Then the question in theology becomes, What "governs" the freedom of God? Before we know it, we are in the dark and unfathomable waters of the purposes of God and the predestination question.

Now, because the second and third generations of English Protestants wished to take to these waters, even to plunge forward into them, the reaction to grace was bound to be quite polar and extreme. The theological reaction, expressed in such otherwise respectable divines as Lancelot Andrewes and Jeremy Taylor, was vigorous. Thus in the name of *anti-Calvinism* was the Protestant face of Anglicanism marred and flecked in the early 1600s.

A *third* reason for the reaction in Stuart England to the Reformation was genetic. Just as Queen Elizabeth had *had* to be a Protestant by virtue of her birth, so James I and his Stuart successors were open to Roman Catholicism because of the "French Connection." The Stuarts were related to the Guises in France, royal Catholic extremists who hated the Reformation to the death. This relation was embodied in Mary Stuart, "Queen of Scots," who *had* to be a Catholic as much as her cousin Elizabeth *had* to be the other. So the Achilles' heel of the Protestant Settlement in England would be, until the exile of the Stuarts in 1688 and their supplanting by the Dutch connection of William of Orange and his Queen Mary, the French relation to Scotland. This was an odd historical paradox given the Scottish *people's* overwhelmingly positive response to Reformed Protestantism. It became an extremely costly paradox over time.

Thus, a reaction to Protestantism set in under James (Stuart) the First of England. Initially, it took the form of theological debates within the University of Cambridge. Then, it moved to episcopal appointments. It advanced soon enough to the appointment of William Laud to Canterbury in 1633, succeeding the outspoken and most unguileful Protestant Archbishop George Abbott (1611-1633). Thereupon, the Catholic reaction overtook the political world, with definite moves towards autonomy under Charles I, moves to consolidate pure power in king and prelates.

The English people, in their vast majority, remained convinced Protestants — not Puritans in the majority, but convinced Protestants. The pot boiled over in 1641: civil war broke out between "King" and "Parliament." The history of England through the entire seventeenth century can be understood as the growing crisis of counter-Protestant moves against the popular Protestant Settlement of Elizabeth, a settlement that had left certain points open and therefore vulnerable to such reaction. If Protestantism in England was for the most part a forward, freeing drift, then Catholicism in England became a backward, reactive undertow. The tide was going out on the Reformation.

Although the reaction to the reaction — which was the English Civil Wars, the deposition of Charles Stuart, his execution in 1649, and the making of England a Commonwealth under Oliver Cromwell as Lord Protector — seemed to be a success for the Protestant cause, it was not so in hindsight. The Protestant face of Anglicanism seemed to be turned towards the colder light (or so it felt) of the Puritan divines. These developed a reputation for self-righteousness and didacticism, even for a spirit of killjoy, which has hung over their reputations ever since. The Commonwealth deprived godly Protestant bishops as well as worldly prelatical ones. The sequestration of Joseph Hall, Bishop of Norwich, for example, in 1643 was entirely arbitrary and counterproductive. Bishop Hall, one of the best and soundest voices the Protestant Church of England ever had, was turned out of house and home purely for the reason that he was a bishop. The Commonwealth *needed* such voices. Not for almost two centuries would Protestant theologians of the quality of Hall, Carleton of Llandaff, and Samuel Ward of Sidney Sussex College, Cambridge, be part of the senior establishment in the Church of England.

After the Lord Protector died in 1658, a fairly exhausted England, represented by some of Cromwell's original best men, called back from France the king in due succession, Charles II. High Church exiles, like the Laudian reactionary John Cosin, returned with him. (They would have lost only their preferments, not their heads, at the hands of the Commonwealth.) The Church of England then turned around and roundly punished the Puritans, ejecting two thousand Puritan clergy from their parishes. One-time Puritan Anglicans now became Puritan Dissenters. The Church lost an important voice, the more fervent Protestant one, forever. Exit John Bunyan and John Milton.

But then again: a reaction to the reaction to the reaction — to the reaction! That is, from the Laudian *reaction* to second-generation Reformation Anglicanism; to the Cromwellian *reaction* to the Laudian reaction; to the Restoration *reaction* to the Cromwellian reaction; and now to the Glorious Revolution: the permanent reaction to the English "counter-reformation."

No sooner had Charles II died in 1688 than his brother, James II, succeeded him. James was a Roman Catholic. In his three years on the throne, he sought with every prerogative he held to restore England to the old religion. On May 16, 1688, his royal efforts to turn the clock back to 1558 were checked by one of the most dramatic events in the history of the English Church. This was the "Petition of the Seven Bishops" (Canterbury, St. Asaph, Bath and Wells, Bristol, Chichester, Ely, and Peterborough) against King James's bill to license the Roman Catholic Church again in England. Scarcely before and never since have bishops of the Church of England so hit a popular nerve than when they faced down the King in the name of the Protestant religion. They were all imprisoned, then they were all released (by order of the courts). Very soon thereafter came the invitation from "the immortal seven" (the Dukes of Shrewsbury, Devonshire, Danby, Lumley; the Bishop of London; Edward Russell and Henry Sidney) to William the Prince of Orange in the Netherlands to become, with his wife Mary (the Protestant daughter of the Catholic James II!), the King and Queen of England. William and Mary arrived in 1688, the event known as the Glorious Revolution, and were crowned as joint monarchs in 1689.

Thus after more than a century and a half of turnings, reactions, and counterreactions, the matter of religion in England was settled, legally and permanently. Parliament's Declaration of Rights of February 13, 1689, and the Act of Settlement of 1701 are the concluding documents relating to the English Reformation:

> Whereas the late King James the Second, by the assistance of divers evil counsellors, judges, and ministers employed by him, did endeavor to subvert and extirpate the Protestant religion and the laws and liberties of the Kingdom. . . .
>
> And whereas the said late King James the Second having abdicated the government, and the throne being thereby vacant, his Highness the Prince of Orange (whom it hath pleased Almighty God to make the glorious instrument of delivering this kingdom from popery and arbitrary power). . . .[12]

---

12. The Declaration of Rights, as quoted on pp. 318-19 of Stuart E. Prall, *The Bloodless Revolution: England 1688* (Madison, 1985), pp. 321-22.

... it was thereby further enacted, that all and every person and persons that then were or afterwards should be reconciled to or shall hold communion with the see or Church of Rome, or should profess the popish religion or marry a papist, . . . are by that Act made forever incapable to inherit, possess or enjoy the crown and government of this realm and Ireland and the Dominions thereunto belonging.[13]

The Protestant face of Anglicanism, now set into enduring legal and constitutional statement, took its final and official form in the Coronation Oath, in which the monarch pledges to defend the Reformed Protestant Church of England by Law Established. Neither the Oath, nor the Declaration of Rights, nor the Act of Settlement has ever been repealed.

In summary, the English Reformation lasted not 40 years (1520-1560) but 170 years (1520-1690). After an ambivalent beginning (Henry VIII); a surge forward (Edward VI); a knock backward (Mary Tudor); a Protestant Settlement, with leaks (Elizabeth I); a "slow-burn" reaction to that Settlement (James I and Charles I); a reaction to the reaction (the Commonwealth period); a reaction to the reaction to the reaction (the Restoration of Charles II); and a final hyper-reactionary episode (James II), the mind of the nation as a whole declared itself in the invitation to William and Mary to become the Protestant King and Queen of England. Their accession was sealed in the Declaration of Rights, the Act of Settlement, and the Coronation Oath. The English Reformation resulted in a Protestant Reformed Church and a Protestant Reformed Nation. To describe the face of Anglicanism in 1668 as anything other than Protestant would be wholly erroneous. As of the turn of the century, the accepted face of Anglicanism was Protestant, without leaks and conditions. The Reformation, with all its snakes and ladders, proved at the end of the day to be the defining moment for Anglican identity.

---

13. The Act of Settlement as quoted in Prall, *The Bloodless Revolution*, p. 322.

CHAPTER 2

The Face Obscured

Parson Thwackum's description of the Church of England in Henry
Fielding's novel *Tom Jones* is axiomatic for a certain commonly held
understanding of Anglicanism in the 1700s. We smile over its pom-
posity and its complacency:

> When I mention religion, I mean the Christian religion, and not
> only the Christian religion, but the Protestant religion; and not
> only the Protestant religion, but the Church of England.[1]

Such a picture of Anglicanism is as far away from the prevailing
understandings as Mars is from Venus. More telling are these more
recent descriptions of the characteristically "Anglican":

> The goal of *via media* is the effort to establish an identity which
> is both Catholic and Reformed, yet in a special sense neither.[2]

> The aim of *via media* was to introduce into religion, and to base
> upon the "light of reason," that love of balance, restraint, mod-

---

1. Henry Fielding, *Tom Jones,* Washington Square Press Edition (New York,
1963), p. 79.
2. Paul Elmen, "Anglican Morality," in *The Study of Anglicanism,* ed. Stephen
Sykes and John Booty (London and Minneapolis, 1988), p. 325.

29

eration, measure, which from sources beyond our reckoning appear to be innate in the English temper. . . .[3] The hallmark of Anglican morality has been the *aurea mediocritas,* the Golden Mean, the measure of nothing too much.[4]

Anglicanism is something that could be shaped to suit one's requirements. . . . Certainly the concept of Anglicanism offers a field day for tendentious interpretations and definitions.[5]

The tacit consensus as to the Protestant character of the Church of England and hence of wider Anglicanism . . . has faded.[6]

There are at least six reasons for this fading of the Protestant character of Anglicanism, or, you could almost say, the scouring away of whatever traces of it are left.

One reason is the association of Protestantism with an *extreme* on the spectrum of worldwide Christianity. On this line, English *Protestantism* is equivalent to English *Puritanism.* We can judge that John Milton, Isaac Watts, and John Bunyan were part of the Puritan movement. Certainly they were not members of the Church of England. Then, too, the earlier voices of the English Reformation, such as those of William Tyndale and Thomas Barnes, were scarcely Anglican because the Church of England had not yet come into being in a settled way. Then there are certain members of the Church of England, such as John Hooper under Edward VI and William Whittingham under Elizabeth, who were consciously Protestant well before they were members of any national Church. Even the great martyrs under Mary, specifically Thomas Cranmer, Nicholas Ridley, and Hugh Latimer, are hard to categorize as Anglicans,[7] for their

---

3. Paul Elmer More and Frank Leslie Cross, eds., *Anglicanism* (London, 1962), p. xxii.

4. Elmen, "Anglican Morality," pp. 325-26.

5. Paul Avis, "What Is 'Anglicanism'?" in *The Study of Anglicanism,* p. 406.

6. Avis, "What Is 'Anglicanism'?" p. 418.

7. "(Cranmer) would not have known what Anglicanism meant, and he would

ministries took place in transitional times, before the settlement of
the 1560s — before the Church knew what it was.

But what did the Church become?

How are we to weigh the conscious Protestantism of every early
Elizabethan bishop, from Aylmer to Jewel to Coxe to Sandys to
Hutton to Grindal to Parker to Parkhurst to Whitgift to Bancroft?
Every one of them, without a single exception, saw himself as a
convinced Protestant as regards theology, not just as a non-Roman
Christian. The overwhelming majority of Anglican bishops under
Elizabeth I and James I were conscious Protestants. This description
was proved beyond the shadow of a doubt in 1849, when the Parker
Society began to publish the collected writings and remains of the
Reformation-era English divines. The massive evidence of conscious
English Protestantism exists to be read in the dark brown volumes
of the Parker Society. It reveals the audacious anachronism of any
interpretation that sees Anglicanism as standing somehow apart
from the Reformation.

Yes, Anglicanism *can* be distinguished from Puritan dissent. It
cannot, however, be distinguished from Protestant self-understanding, at least not until very recently and in any case anachronistically.

A *second reason* for the obscuring of the Protestant face of Anglicanism is the charge of Calvinism. If Calvinism is understood as
an expression of the overly systematic in religion, and specifically as
the assertion of the decrees of God over against the will of men, and
even more specifically as the declaration of double predestination
within God's ultimate plan for the human race, then Calvinism is
an obvious enemy to human flourishing.

The English Reformers of the sixteenth century were for the
most part (the exceptions being Tyndale, Frith, Bilney, and Barnes)
closer to the Reformed, or Calvinistic, strand of European Protes-

---

probably not have approved if the meaning had been explained to him, but without
his contribution *the unending dialogue of Protestantism and Catholicism which forms
Anglican identity* would not have been possible" (italics added).

See Diarmaid MacCulloch, *Thomas Cranmer* (New Haven and London, 1996),
p. 629.

tantism than they were to the Lutheran. Dean Litton demonstrated this in his 1882 *Theology*. His demonstration is a certainty in relation to those of the Thirty-Nine Articles that speak of the Sacrament of Holy Communion. The Cambridge historian Patrick Collinson describes the Church of England's relation to Calvinism as follows:

> The time has come to acknowledge that there was a . . . broadly-based reception of Calvinism in the Elizabethan and Jacobean Church of England. . . . It has often been said that the Church of England is not a confessional church. Nevertheless, the account of salvation, faith, grace, and predestination rendered by the Articles was broadly consistent with the Reformed consensus on these matters. . . . We concede that the Church of England was putting down its anchors in the outer roads of the broad harbours of the Calvinist or [better] Reformed Tradition.[8]

Despite these facts of the matter, historically speaking, there is today a no more frightful and damaging epithet for an Episcopalian to receive than that of "Calvinist." It was not long ago that a national evangelism officer for the American Episcopal Church dismissed a famous and highly honored Church of England dignitary as a "Calvinist." It was the kiss of death. No more would this good man from across the sea be invited back to speak or to consult. This writer questioned the justice, let alone the accuracy, of the charge. "Well," the officer replied, "He is an Evangelical, and aren't all Evangelicals Calvinists?" "Prithee, what is a Calvinist?" "A Calvinist is a fundamentalist!" And so went the conversation. Whatever "Calvinist" means, and not withstanding the historic importance of Calvinism as a vital factor in the coming to birth of the Church of England, to be a "Calvinist" is apparently to be the worst sort of fundamentalist maggot.

Thus the Protestant face of Anglicanism is scarred by the accusa-

---

8. Patrick Collinson, "England and International Calvinism 1558-1640," in *International Calvinism 1541-1715*, ed. Menna Prestwich (Oxford, 1985), pp. 213, 215.

tion of "Calvinist." Correlative to this is the disassociation of any notion of the *bound will* from Anglicanism as it is now understood. We have all become cheerleaders for the concept of "free will." We no more envision or recognize the limits placed on human freedom by the world, the flesh, and the devil. In the case of the "free will" question, we have probably become the prisoners of current notions of personal autonomy as *summum bonum* or highest good. An unrestrained practical notion of free will is another price paid by Anglicanism to the total erasure of "Calvinism" from the Anglican profile.

A *third reason* for the obscuring of the Protestant face of Anglicanism lies in the charges against it of moralism, consistency, stringency, and self-righteousness; or more crudely, the charge of *inhumanity*. Review any standard text on European or American history, on European or American literature, or on European or American religious history in particular, and you will encounter words like "dour," "stout," "grim," and "hardy"; "rugged," "austere," "determined," "sober," and, in a lower key, "harsh"; "strict," "straight-laced," and "unyielding," used to describe Protestants and Protestantism. It would be very hard, in fact, to find a contemporary portrayal of Protestants in literature *qua* their Protestantism that did not describe them in these terms. The progression of association travels thus: Protestant religion is Bible-religion; hence it is ideological religion; hence it is systematic religion; hence it is unswerving, inflexible, narrow-minded religion; hence it is dogmatic, sermonic, intolerant religion; hence it is self-righteous religion; hence it is moralizing religion; hence it is control religion; hence it is autocracy and oligarchy; hence it is finally despotism; hence it is murder.

A case in point of this extreme but fairly common progression of associations is the "counterfactual" portrayal of John Milton in Peter Ackroyd's recent novel *Milton in America*. *This* Milton, Peter Ackroyd's Milton, very unhistorically flees from England to New England in the year 1660, where he establishes a settlement called New Milton. There he becomes increasingly tyrannical until he ultimately leads the "Puritans" in a war of extermination against neighboring Roman Catholics. One reviewer of the book wrote,

Now, the Puritans are easy to hate, and we are all too familiar with what dreadful things they did, what deranged perversities their imaginations were capable of. . . . But (Mr. Ackroyd's) frontal attack on the Puritans is blunt and coarse; the points he scores against them are embarrassingly cheap and easy. . . . It comes across as pastiche with one point: to make Puritans appear as mad, cruel and all-round hateful as possible.[9]

The root of this tireless charge against Protestant religion, which is usually branded as "Puritan," "Calvinist," and "patriarchal" by definition, may lie in the original Reformed or Calvinist definition of "church," by which "church discipline" and the *form* of the church are as important defining characteristics as "the true Word of God preached" and the "Sacraments duly administered according to Christ's ordinance" (Article XIX of the Thirty-Nine Articles). The Lutherans and Anglicans restricted the identifying marks of the "church" to the last two. The Reformed or Calvinist branch of the Reformation added "godly order" and discipline as marks of the true church. So *order* and *discipline,* hence *morality,* became of equal weight in practice with the religious value of right teaching and preaching, and the sacraments of Baptism and Holy Communion. Thus there came into being the Reformation's sterner face, calling for "order" as well as for "doctrine." This sterner face, which appeared and in fact grew to be ever more legalistic, has come in the popular mind to stand for the entire Protestant profile. It is only a part of the picture, in fact, and a very small part of the picture in respect to Protestant Anglicanism itself.

Even so, even within the more extreme sections of Reformed Protestantism, there are fundamental exceptions of which the picture of Protestantism as *inhumane* takes no account. There is the genre of Puritan hymns and poems to married love; there is the attitude of all the Reformers to clerical marriage; there are the liberalized views of divorce that opened up in the sixteenth century; there is

9. Tony Tanner, review of *Milton in America*, in *The New York Times,* April 6, 1997, p. 14.

the painting of seventeenth-century Holland and the music of the North German baroque; and there is the bloom of Tudor literature in the "Calvinist" climate of late Elizabethan England. Words fail, for there are so many counterexamples to the *opinio communis* that Protestantism is stringent, ideological, and finally inhumane. A sublime text for this counterpoint is Denis de Rougemont's book *Love in the Western World.*[10]

In the case of Anglicanism, the *charge* against Protestantism as being morbidly systematic, hence inhumane, has had the effect of freeing "Anglican" thought from the obligation to be consistent or thorough. To be "Anglican" means rather to be formed from *praxis*, not principle; from *context*, not idea; from *ethos*, not content. "If we are looking for a single term to denote the ultimate case of Anglicanism, I do not see that we can do better than adopt a title which offers itself as peculiarly descriptive. . . . I refer to the title 'Pragmatism.'"[11] In other words, Anglicans are liberated from having to think!

We see that the Protestant face of Anglicanism has been obscured, or worn down, by the removal of the Puritan, the Calvinist, and the "inhumane" associations. This means that what has happened over time is the creation of a portrait by *negation*. It is what Anglicanism is *not*, rather than what Anglicanism *is*, that has determined the interpretation. Now definition by negation is never a happy solution to the problem of identity. Definition by negation involves reaction and a shrinking from, rather than affirmation or confident assertion. Restoring the Protestant face of Anglicanism, by contrast, will be an exercise in affirmation rather than negation, of addition (based on traditions that *have* been there all along but have been overlooked or neglected) and enhancement. Anglicanism as negation reveals itself to be a highly defined and restricted, tiny and slight, tightly bounded sliver of traditional Christianity.

There is more to the negative, to the "axe laid to the root of the tree" of Protestant Anglicanism, than we have seen so far. A *fourth*

10. Denis de Rougemont, *Love in the Western World* (Princeton, 1956).
11. Paul Elmer More in *Anglicanism*, p. xxxii.

cause of the Protestant effacement in governing notions of Anglican identity is the belief that "Anglicanism" is based on synthesis rather than antithesis. A. M. Allchin expressed this notion in his 1988 essay entitled "Anglican Spirituality," with its "insistence that all things created can be loved in and for God . . . [the Anglican] longing to gather together the fullness of the created order in all its diversity, into the unity of the kingdom."[12] There is also a drift here to the concept of truth as *the reconciliation of opposites for its own sake.* The danger here is easy accommodation. We are not speaking of Christian charity and the accommodation of "otherness." We are not speaking of Christian love and acceptance of "the other." We are speaking of an urge to deny the conflict of ideas. We are speaking of an unwillingness to confront the contradiction of premises. This is an area where Anglicanism has been notoriously weak, even timorous. We have been reluctant to think systematically about theology; therefore we think scarcely at all! The intellectual process requires the setting out of theses or propositions, and antitheses or counterpropositions. In the weighing of the two, through investigation and debate, elements of truth as well as falsehood become clear. The scientific method *requires* antithetical thinking — even if some sort of synthetic solution be the ultimate goal. But when balance and moderation *as such* are overly valued at the starting gate, fact and counterfact cannot be established. The tendency to wish to argue synthetically from the start, almost as a salute to "Englishness" or some aesthetic notion of *aureus mediocritas,* is a faulty one. It excludes from Anglicanism the values and fruits of science, reducing us, again, to an ethos or tone. Process becomes dominant over conclusion. Thus the Protestant face of Anglicanism has been effaced by a synthetic method that has issued in an implicit anti-intellectualism. It is no surprise that almost all of the few systematic treatments of Christian theology undertaken by Anglicans, outside of the Thirty-Nine Articles themselves, have come from the Protestant schools of thought within the Church.

A *fifth cause* of erosion caused to the Protestant profile of Angli-

12. In *The Study of Anglicanism,* p. 324.

canism is the notion that Anglican religion starts with the incarnation rather than the atonement. This view goes back to the nineteenth-century Oxford Movement, which was a reaction in part to the overly facile use of atonement and cross-centered imagery by the Evangelicals. At that time the Evangelicals were the vocal and ascending power within the Church. The Tractarians, as the Oxford Movement Anglicans came to be called, were so repelled by the easy reduction of Christianity to a simple monocular preaching of the cross, often to the end only of personal conversion, that they became attracted, *by reaction,* to versions of believing that emphasized the incarnation.

It is certainly true that there are two possible Christologies, or views of Christ and his work, within the Christian religion: an atonement Christology and an incarnation Christology. The first lays primary emphasis on Christ the Savior: Christ the Pardoner of sins. The second lays primary emphasis on Christ the Sympathizer: Christ the One who shared our lot, our life, our nature, thus also our sorrow and our pain. Eastern Orthodox Christianity makes great cause over the aspect of this second Christology by which Christ "divinizes" the world in lifting all things unto or into himself. This notion is abstract, contemplating as it does the "divinization of all things." The church historian von Harnack spied within the Eastern Orthodox emphasis elements of classical antiquity, specifically the notion that human beings could be wholly divinized, partly divinized, or translated to heaven in a godly epiphany. However we judge the theological concept that the divine became human so that the human could become divine, it is a philosophical, even a metaphysical concept. It is not concrete and will not "preach." The Christology which starts from the incarnation has the advantage of sympathy but will not in itself cut the Gordian knot of human bondage to guilt and stress. *That* job the atonement emphasis is able to do.

The historic point remains, however we weight the two approaches. Atonement, hence the cross, as the starting point, even as the central emphasis in theology, is generally understood to be "Protestant." Incarnation, on the other hand, as the starting point or central emphasis is generally understood to be "Catholic." The in-

37

carnation is often claimed to be the Anglican emphasis in theology. On this claim, the Protestant profile is once again further effaced. The cross is not at the top of the agenda. Issues of guilt's transference or transfer, issues of the efficacy of sacrifice and the blood of Christ, the portrayal of Christianity as primarily a religion of *salvation:* these things become secondary. Here is a fundamental erosion of the Protestant face of Anglicanism: the elimination of the cross as the central theme. Cross-centered Christologies and theologies, therefore, are depicted as Protestant, distinct from Anglican; as Evangelical, distinct from Catholic; as either-or as distinct from both-and; as once-and-for-all as opposed to process; as sanctification-oriented as opposed to justification-oriented. With tunnel vision on the incarnation, Anglican theology would become, in material terms, a subset of Roman Catholic theology.

A *sixth reason* for the collapse of Protestant confidence within Anglicanism is the charge that Protestantism *secularizes,* while Catholicism is *really* religious. This is the line according to which Protestant Christianity stresses so much the unmediated relation of God with man that it knocks away the instruments of mediation such as priesthood, liturgy as an end in itself, and implicitly the Church as the "continuing incarnation," visible to the here and now, of the Christ of God. This charge caused John Newman to leave the Anglican Church for the Church of Rome. He saw the Protestant impulse as finally irreligious.

There is justice in this charge to the extent that Protestant ideality — God and man "face to face," the veil of the temple rent in twain, the collapse of mediation as a principle in religion — requires renewal in every generation and within every human being. It cannot be passed down by means of "things" or instruments. It is ever dynamic, even arduously so. Protestantism is only irreligious if irreligion describes Christianity without veils.

The result of the sixfold effacement of the Protestant profile of Anglican Christianity is a narrowing of focus that has created an "Anglican" identity which threatens to become no longer universal, nor existentially penetrating, nor emotionally animating. This sixfold abridgement of the Anglican band on the spectrum of believing threatens to render it nonprofound.

In the first place, it unchurches the Puritan trend towards systematization, thereby loosing from itself the value of thorough analysis altogether. In the second place, it unchurches the Calvinist emphasis on the immanence of Providence, that is, the biblical conviction of God's active relation to all contingency and eventuality and *happening* in the world. In the third place, it unchurches seriousness in religion. It thereby tends to become trivial, or, rather, focused on penultimate rather than ultimate aspects of Christianity. This tendency to trivialize creates the impression that Anglicanism is superficial. In the fourth place, it unchurches the scientific method of proposing antitheses to discover truth and facticity. In the fifth place, it shuffles off the requirement of having to give an account of the cross of Christ, thereby letting go of the primary question, the *salvation* question. The tilt towards a theology which begins with incarnation stresses process and presence rather than crisis and release. In the sixth place, it becomes deaf to the secular yet authentic cry for unmediated communication in the relation of God and humanity.

What is left of the identity of Anglicanism after this sixfold effacement of the Protestant profile? Is Paul Avis right to describe the present situation as "a nerveless failure to grapple with Christian truth systematically"?[13] Or is it really "pragmatism" that defines the Anglican way? Or do we wish to punt back, with O. C. Edwards, to the Prayer Book?[14] That is a particularly shaky move now, as the Prayer Book has undergone frequent revision since achieving its definitive form, in England at least, in 1662. Moreover, revision of the Prayer Book has proliferated in many provinces of the Communion. It is now without doubt impossible to answer any given question concerning Anglicanism by answering it with the question that

13. See his "What is 'Anglicanism'?" p. 422.

14. O. C. Edwards quotes Roger Lord approvingly in his essay "Anglican Pastoral Tradition," in *The Study of Anglicanism*, p. 342: "It is in the Prayer Book that we find the heart of Anglicanism laid bare."

used to be able to settle almost everything: What does the Prayer Book say about this?!

Are the remains of Anglican identity to be located in *ethos*, or in "Englishness" — romantically conceived of as moderation and balance — or in deliberate fuzziness as representing the character of truth? Are we in fact staring at a wax nose?

One thing we *can* say concerning current Anglican identity. Whatever it remains in itself, it has become a small slice, a bounded band, along the spectrum of historic Christianity. Without any of the above Protestant features, which in fact sustained and supported it in the past, it becomes a form of liberal Catholicism *from the outside* (i.e., the clergy usually look like Catholic priests and act like Catholic priests in the act of worship itself), with deeply inset and encased views about secondary issues *on the inside*. Anglicans today, living within the narrow band of negation (i.e., what we are *not*), tend towards an astonishing absolutism concerning secondary questions. The church of incarnation, synthesis, and Englishness strangely attaches the same degree of importance that our forebears once attached to issues like atonement and justification, to issues of liturgical correctness, not to mention political issues from the world's ever-changing store. The wax nose is chameleon! It may take only a return to the Protestant profile, a review of what used to exist in the Church as ballast and solid freight, to set things on a sure foundation again.

What exactly *has* been the Protestant profile of Anglicanism in the past? What are we missing, the reappropriation of which might be sufficient to reendow us with weight and substance? Is there a solution to the chronic problem of superficiality? It is not so much a problem of having poor content, but rather of having insubstantial content. Restoring the Protestant profile is part of the needed task of strengthening the *content* of our faith. As it stands now, we are simply too weak to attract the seriously *needy* as well as the seriously *thoughtful*. The seriously *needy* will gravitate to the independent and charismatic churches. The seriously *thoughtful* will continue to gravitate towards Roman Catholicism. Do we really wish to be a *way-station*? Or can we find the means to restore our confidence such that we become a terminus?

CHAPTER 3

The Protestant Face of Anglicanism in the Church of England (1688 to the Present)

J. C. Ryle described the early and middle years of the eighteenth century as one of the low ebbs of Christian history in England:

> The state of this country in a religious and moral point of view in the middle of the last century was so painfully unsatisfactory that it is difficult to convey any adequate idea of it . . . Christianity seemed to lie as one dead, insomuch that you might have said "she is dead." . . . Does anyone ask what the churches were doing a hundred years ago? The answer is soon given. Natural Theology, without a single distinctive doctrine of Christianity, cold morality, or barren orthodoxy, formed the staple teaching both in church and chapel. Sermons everywhere were little better than miserable moral essays. . . . And as for the mighty truths for which Hooper and Latimer had gone to the stake, and Baxter and scores of Puritans had gone to jail, they seemed clean forgotten and laid on the shelf.[1]

1. J. C. Ryle, *Christian Leaders of the Eighteenth Century* (Edinburgh and Carlisle, Pa., 1978), p. 14.

It could not have been that bad! Sincere Christian writers were producing devotional books that sold, church attendance was in fact steady and high, a kind of stoical but well-intentioned faith reigned, primarily through the influence of the sermons of Archbishop Til-lotson. The very last gasp of resistance to Protestant rule in England ended with the defeat on the battlefield of the Jacobite (i.e., Stuart) Pretender come over from France.

Yet the fact remains that as a whole the Church was lacking in *feeling*. The Church of England lacked "religious affections," as one would have said then, and there was indeed a hunger for living religion. The existence of this hunger is demonstrated by subsequent events.

On May 24, 1738, John Wesley felt his "heart strangely warmed" and soon professed conversion. A clerk in Anglican orders, Wesley received assurance of forgiveness and a new beginning in Christ. This was after years of painful searching and in the immediate aftermath of an episode at Savannah, Georgia, which revealed a man of perilously little self-knowledge and the tendency to hypocrisy. Wesley *caught* these things in himself. He felt *caught* by Christ and pardoned. With John Wesley's turning the Evangelical Revival began.

Wesley, together with his brother Charles; the evangelist with a bit of genius, George Whitefield; various clergy who experienced conversion in out-of-the-way ministries (Samuel Walker, William Grimshaw, Henry Venn, William Romaine, John Berridge, Joseph Milner, John Newton, Thomas Adam, John Fletcher, Daniel Row-lands, Augustus Montague Toplady, Thomas Scott, James Hervey, and several others, all curates or vicars in remote parishes far from the metropolis of London, Romaine's parish being the exception); and certain converted laymen in high places, such as the Countess of Huntingdon and Lord Dartmouth: these people were gripped by a faith rivaled only by the force of conviction the Reformers had had.

Viewed as pariahs and mavericks, later as schismatics (John Wes-ley on his side — the *anti-Calvinist* evangelicals — and Countess Selina Huntingdon on her side — the *Calvinist* evangelicals), and always as evincing much too much intensity about religion, these early "evangelicals," as they began to be called, created a sea change in England, and in particular within the Church of England.

Those "evangelicals" who remained loyal members of the Church of England formed that connection of common-minded clergy and laity which within two generations had become the Evangelical party within the Church of England. With the strategic visionary thinking of Charles Simeon (1759-1836) and with the parallel visionary leadership of aristocratic patrons like William Wilberforce, Henry Thornton, and the others known as the Clapham Sect (because they owned houses abutting Clapham Common in the north London suburbs), the Evangelicals succeeded — slowly — in being appointed to "town" parishes, Oxbridge professorships, and finally, in 1815, to the Episcopal bench. The first Evangelical bishop was Henry Ryder, Bishop of Gloucester. The first Evangelical Archbishop of Canterbury was John Bird Sumner, appointed in 1848. In addition to the important spheres of influence in the Church now opened to them, the Evangelicals succeeded, against all odds (as seen *at the time*), in getting slavery outlawed in the British Empire and in getting industrial legislation passed which greatly alleviated the plight of the working poor.

The novelist George Eliot described in 1858 the effects of Evangelical Anglicanism on one small and archetypical English village:

> Evangelicalism was making its way in Milby, and gradually diffusing its subtle odour into chambers that were bolted and barred against it. . . . It may be that some of Mr. Tryan's hearers had gained a religious vocabulary rather than religious experience; that here and there a weaver's wife, who, a few months before, had been simply a silly slattern, was converted into that more complex nuisance, a silly and sanctimonious slattern; that the old Adam, with the pertinacity of middle age, continued to tell fibs behind the counter, notwithstanding the new Adam's addiction to Bible-reading and family prayer; that the children in the Paddiford Sunday-school had their memories crammed with phrases about the blood of cleansing, imputed righteousness, and

justification by faith alone, which an experience lying principally in . . . hop-scotch, parental slappings, and longings after unattainable lollipop, served rather to darken than to illustrate; and that at Milby, in those distant days, as in all other times and places where the mental atmosphere is changing, and men are inhaling the stimulus of new ideas, folly often mistook itself for wisdom, ignorance gave itself airs of knowledge, and selfishness, turning its eyes upward, called itself religion.

Nevertheless, Evangelicalism had brought into palpable existence and operation in Milby society that idea of duty, that recognition of something to be lived far beyond the mere satisfaction of self, which is to the moral life what the addition of a great central ganglion is to animal life. . . . The first condition of human goodness is something to love; the second, something to reverence. And this latter precious gift was bought to Milby by Mr. Tryan and Evangelicalism.[2]

As a result of the Evangelical Revival, the Protestant face of the Church of England became, practically speaking, the face of its Evangelical constituency. It was the Evangelicals who gloried in the Thirty-Nine Articles and the Reformation Homilies and in the Book of Common Prayer as the doctrinal exposition of what they so deeply felt in their hearts. Charles Simeon of Cambridge expressed for all time the intersection of the Protestant foundation documents of Anglicanism with the mission fervor of his Evangelical school of thought:

The Bible first, the Prayer Book next, and all other books and doings in subordination to both.

The difference between the Church spirit and the sectarian spirit is very much owing to the prayers of the Church being

2. George Eliot, *Scenes of Clerical Life*, Penguin World's Classics (Oxford, 1988), pp. 227-28.

fixed and commanding, and full of the things requisite for every sinner.

The finest sight short of heaven would be a whole congregation using the prayers of the liturgy in the true spirit of them.[3]

It is also true that a Protestant understanding of Anglicanism remained strong among many clergy and laity who did not see themselves as Evangelicals. E. A. Litton is an example of a Protestant Church of England theologian who did not consider himself an Evangelical. But theologically speaking, non-Evangelical Protestant Anglicans and Evangelical Protestant Anglicans were joined in most matters of theology. They would soon make common cause against Tractarianism or the Oxford Movement. The Evangelicals may have been the cutting edge of Protestant Anglicanism, but they were not the whole constituency.

An important glimpse into the Protestant self-understanding of the vast majority of English people at mid-century is crystalized in a letter of Queen Victoria to Dean Wellesley in 1866. The Queen wrote this letter after the Episcopal Church of Scotland, in militant competition with the Established Church of Scotland, which was presbyterian in government, had begun building an Episcopal cathedral at Inverness. The Queen saw the Scottish Episcopal Church's *implication*, that the Established Church was no true church because it did not have bishops, as sectarian and narrow-minded:

> The Queen considers this [Episcopalian] movement as *most* mischievous. The Presbyterian Church is essentially *Protestant*, and, as such, *most* valuable. The Reformation in this country was *never* fully completed, and had we applied the pruning knife more severely, we should *never* have been exposed to the dangers to which the Church of England is *now* exposed. . . .
>
> The Queen feels, *more strongly* than words *can* express, the duty which is imposed upon her and her family, to maintain the

3. As quoted by Charles Smyth in *Simeon and Church Order* (Cambridge, 1940), pp. 291, 292.

true and *real principle* and *spirit* of the *Protestant* religion; . . . and the Queen will *not* stand the attempts made to destroy the simple and truly Protestant faith of the Church of Scotland, and to bring the Church of England as near the Church of Rome as they possibly can.[4] (All italics are original.)

The Evangelical party within the Church of England was the high and sharp profile of Anglican Protestantism during the nineteenth century, as it remains today. But the pulling in of Protestant consciousness to the Evangelical group more or less alone was the later result of the Oxford or Tractarian Movement. The Oxford Movement or "Church Revival" campaigned so aggressively to occupy the high ground of Church identity in England that it effectively pushed back into a corner the broad Protestant consensus that had existed before it. That corner was the Evangelical constituency within the Church, which by the early twentieth century had through this "twist of fate" (i.e., the success of the Oxford Movement) become a small and dismissed, even a despised minority. How was this revolution, almost another change of religion for the Church of England, achieved?

The Oxford Movement, the beginning of which is marked by John Keble's 1833 sermon in the Church of St. Mary the Virgin, Oxford, entitled "National Apostasy," was an intellectual and aesthetic replay of the sixteenth-century Counter-Reformation. It lacked only the Tudor mind-set according to which heretics deserved death rather than contempt. We have seen that Queen Elizabeth's Protestant Settlement had left holes or "windows of vulnerability" in the final form achieved by the Reformation in England as of 1653. These holes or gaps had been exploited by catholicizing elements, from Laud's anti-Calvinism to King Charles's anti-republicanism to King James II's anti-Protestantism. A loyal lid had been placed over all such exploitations by virtue of the Hanoverian accession of 1688. But the internal conflict, endemic to Elizabeth's incomplete "solution" of the original Reformation crisis, simmered. An incipient

4. *Letters of Queen Victoria*, Second Series: 1862-78, 1:376-78.

high-churchmanship and an inward repulsion against Protestant theologies of grace and divine sovereignty were factors in English life, low profile as they were. We can see this, for example, in the particular churchmanship of Dr. Samuel Johnson, who, although he was a conscious Protestant, abhorred all Dissenters and Evangelicals, and seemed to long for an authoritarian Tory churchmanship that would *command* all Englishmen to attend the Established Church. Dr. Johnson definitely retained the theocratic impulse.

When J. H. Newman, E. B. Pusey, and John Keble, all of whom had been members of Oriel College, Oxford, in the 1820s (and where E. A. Litton would be dean in the 1840s!), discovered one another and the Catholic heritage of the medieval pre-Reformation Church, they banded together. They launched their celebrated cycle of *Tracts for the Times*. The presenting symptom for them was two things: a government bill to reduce the number of bishoprics in the Church of Ireland and a State-Church initiative to establish an episcopate in Palestine *co*-sponsored with the Lutheran Church of Germany. What the Tractarians, as they came to be called, abhorred was the idea that the government of England should set Church policy in any way, and, worse, that the second move affirmed the *official* Protestant status of the Church of England. The Oxford Tractarians wanted to go back to the days of Henry II and Archbishop Thomas à Becket, in which the Church had *won* against the State and in which the Church was identified across Europe with the theocratic and aesthetic traditions of a uniform and exquisite medieval Catholicism. They saw Protestantism as "national" rather than international (i.e., Roman); as biblical rather than traditional; as implicitly liberal rather than conservative; as republican and "Whig" rather than paternalistic; as implicitly antinomian rather than hierarchical; as iconoclastic rather than adoring; as overly explicit in regard to sacred things, rather than reserved and subtle; and as vulgar if not crude, rather than refined. The Oxford Movement opposed the Reformation tradition root and branch and saw it as the seedbed of secularism and liberalism. The Oxford Movement was intentionally and consciously in reaction. Fortunately for its own ends, the reactionary character of the Movement coincided brilliantly with a general cultural trend to Romanticism, which tended to idealize the Middle Ages.

After 1840, the Oxford Movement split in two sections. Newman moved in an increasingly Catholic direction and in 1845 became a convert to Rome. Many joined him, including H. E. Manning, who went from being Archdeacon of Chichester in the Church of England to being the Roman Catholic Cardinal of all England. The section of Tractarians who remained in the Church of England became the "Anglo-Catholic" party, which still exists today.

The Anglo-Catholic party within the Church struck a nerve, with its medievalism, apparent innovations, such as private confession and frequent observance of Holy Communion, and several other liturgical reversions to supposed pre-Reformation practice. Incidentally, the pre-Reformation Church in England was far less systematic and unitary than the Anglo-Catholics sought to picture it. Legal challenges to Anglo-Catholic practices from Protestants in the Church, leading so far as to the imprisonment of several Anglo-Catholic priests for extreme Roman use, gave the Movement the glow of martyrdom. A certain luster was added to this by the devoted efforts of Anglo-Catholic priests in the blue-collar or working-class East End of London. These men achieved successes for the Church of England among a constituency, the "working man," which only Methodism, 150 years earlier, had been able to achieve. Color and pageantry, the appeal to antiquity, the mystique of "martyrdom," and a social-gospel dimension gave the Anglo-Catholic party an appeal that won them friends in high places. They triumphed in 1928 with the appointment of Cosmo Lang as Archbishop of Canterbury. Lang wore a miter during his consecration — the first time an archbishop had worn a miter since Cranmer discarded his during the reign of Edward VI.

Gradually, Anglo-Catholic liturgy and Anglo-Catholic surfaces became the general rule within the Church of England. Only the Evangelicals, who had been discredited by their attempts legally to challenge the Oxford Movement, remained self-conscious Protestants. Although the foundation documents of Anglicanism, that is, the 1662 Prayer Book, the Edwardian Homilies, and the Thirty-

Nine Articles of Religion, were definitely Protestant, the Articles were increasingly neglected, the Homilies almost entirely forgotten, and the Prayer Book twisted and torn by practical usage contrary to its original letter and spirit.

The final crisis for the Evangelicals came with the Anglo-Catholic initiative to decommission the 1662 Book of Common Prayer and substitute a new book, the Proposed Prayer Book of 1928. In February 1927, during the final tenure of Randall Davidson as Archbishop of Canterbury, the bishops, backed by a majority of the clergy, who were by now strongly under the influence of the Tractarian Movement, presented a new Prayer Book to the Convocations of York and Canterbury. This Prayer Book allowed for several catholicizing innovations in the liturgy, such as the reservation of the Blessed Sacrament and prayers for the dead. But the center point was a refashioning of the service of Holy Communion. The service was altered to be much closer to the *1549* (as opposed to the 1552) Prayer Book. The tilt was definitely to the Catholic side. The proposed Book passed the Church Assembly on July 6, 1927, passed the House of Lords, and was then given to the House of Commons.

In the House of Commons the Book was *defeated*, twice, first in 1927, then again in 1928. It was defeated almost entirely through the brilliant parliamentary and rhetorical efforts of two senior Evangelical Anglican laymen, Sir William Joynson-Hicks and Sir Thomas Inskip. These two men served the Protestant cause in the Church of England. Here is a passage from one of Joynson-Hicks's speeches:

> Those who have been brought up on the Book of Common Prayer [1662] . . . would not wish to be offered a change of doctrine and hate the idea of any alteration being made in that one part of the service of all others, the Service of Holy Communion, which will bring it nearer to the medieval ideas which were abolished for us at the time of the Reformation.[5]

5. Quoted by Randle Manwaring in *From Controversy to Co-Existence: Evangelicals in the Church of England 1914-1980* (Cambridge, 1985), p. 32.

On the last day of parliamentary debate over the proposed book, Sir Thomas Inskip, speaking of "the real tug-of-war . . . about that part of the Book, small in volume but supremely important, connected with the service of Holy Communion,"[6] rose to address the House:

> I feel that this is a grave moment for the House of Commons. This House is going to write its name in history in a few minutes. Still for a few minutes we are asked to defend or to yield what some of us believe to be one of the ramparts of our national faith.[7]

Such "eloquent, gentle but firm persuasiveness" produced a vote against the proposed Prayer Book with a majority of 33. The following year, a second attempt to pass the Book resulted in a larger defeat, with a majority of 46. The Church establishment was staggered and stunned. The Evangelicals were crucified. Labeled as "an army of illiterates, generalled by octogenarians,"[8] they were now to be denied preferment in the Church, stereotyped as ignorant and old-fashioned, thoroughly out of step with the modern spirit (which, so far as classic Anglo-Catholicism is concerned, was not modern at all, but rather romantic, illiberal, and pervasively reactionary), and effectively denied the name of "Anglican."

In the short term, the parliamentary defeat by the Evangelicals of the 1928 proposed Book of Common Prayer marked a half-century nadir of their position and status in the Church of England. In the long run, however, their successful struggle, which secured them only contempt and mockery at the time, maintained the *appearance* at least of the Protestant face of Anglicanism. Had the new Prayer Book passed, the Evangelicals would have mostly departed the Church, somewhat in the way the Puritan clergy were ejected from it in 1662. Such was the fate of American Episcopal Evangelicals after the "Cummins schism" of 1873, which resulted in the formation of the

6. Manwaring, *From Controversy to Co-Existence*, p. 32.
7. Manwaring, *From Controversy to Co-Existence*, p. 33.
8. The remark is attributed to Bishop Hensley Henson of Durham.

Reformed Episcopal Church. Fortunately for Protestant Anglicans in England, the 1928 Book was defeated and the 1662 Book saved. Had the 1928 Book gone through, the Evangelicals would have departed and there would have been no order to carry forward Protestant identity in the Church. Looking back now, Inskip and Joynson-Hicks deserve the enduring gratitude of all who value the Protestant and also the Evangelical element within Anglicanism.

What was a short-term disaster for the Evangelical group, extending right up to the Keele Congress of 1967, was really a long-term victory, the fruits of which we can see today on almost every side. Like all church controversies, the Prayer Book debates of 1927 and of 1928 possessed elements of ego, power politics, posturing, and what theology calls original sin (i.e., human nature evenly distributed). Archbishop Davidson's speeches come across today as patronizing; the bishops as a whole seem smug; the Evangelicals seem extremely worried, and the parliamentary heavy hitters, at times calculating. Perhaps a fitting close to this treatment of the Evangelicals' last-ditch stand, which was ultimately a powerful victory, is the present writer's observing a footnote to history in a television documentary broadcast in 1996 concerning the Beatles. Liverpool, on the Mersey River, was described as a working-class stronghold. Old films of Liverpool's blue-collar slums were shown. Just in the corner of an extended shot of a row of brick houses from the 1920s could be plainly seen a white banner hanging out from the second floor of a tenement. On the banner were painted the words, "Vote 'No' to the 1928 Prayer Book"!

After 1928, the Evangelicals, whose character was now assassinated in the minds of most churchmen, especially those at the deanery, archdiaconal, and episcopal level, let alone at Lambeth Palace, retreated into their parishes, their influence having been nullified on the national scene. But they still had the Protestant Prayer Book and they could still carry on their work. Their influence for good on the local scene remained as strong as ever.

After 1928, the state of the Protestant profile of the Church of

England becomes exactly equivalent to the fortunes of the Evangelical Party. This was not true a century earlier, when the overwhelming majority of Church people, lay and clergy, saw themselves as Protestants, whereas only a very few would not have hidden their faces from the epithet "Evangelical." But since 1928, Protestant identity, explicitly at least, was restricted to the Evangelical sector.

The three watershed dates for Evangelicals since 1928, and thus the three watershed dates for the Protestant profile, are the 1956 London Billy Graham Crusade; the first National Evangelical Anglican Conference in 1967; and the appointment of George Carey as Archbishop of Canterbury in 1991.

The legendary Haringay Crusade of 1956 created an astonishing sensation in England, and especially in the Church of England. American Episcopalians, who are apt to associate Dr. Graham with fundamentalism and the Southern Baptists, are often surprised to learn how profound an impression he made on everyday English people, and not just on Evangelical Christians in general but on Evangelical Anglicans in particular. Many professions of faith from that one crusade became vocations to the Anglican ministry. Many present-day bishops and archdeacons date their entry into the Church precisely from their response to that single crusade. Another important effect of Billy Graham was on the still-embattled Evangelical minority within the Church itself. The apparent free and outgoing style of the American evangelist and his team was new to his Anglican counterparts. A kind of refreshing open spirit poured in upon the English. Certain social barriers, such as a relatively extreme conservatism in manners and fashion, came down overnight. A certain social tension, characteristic of its defensive self-understanding since 1928, relaxed. This was very noticeable at the time.

The second watershed date for the Protestant, now Evangelical, profile of the Church of England was the first National Evangelical Anglican Conference in 1967 held at the University of Keele. It was at this conference that the leadership of John Stott came to the fore within the party. There was a new confidence, and also a new desire to work within the given structures of the Church of England. Keele marked a transition from the siege mentality of post-1928 Anglican

Evangelicalism to a general desire to move beyond that. The result was a strong movement towards diocesan involvement, and, by extension, national involvement.

The work of Colin Buchanan on the Church of England Liturgical Commission dates from this period. Bishop Buchanan's commitment to the wider Church, yet as a convinced Evangelical, is just one of many witnesses to the new churchmanship and muscle of the Evangelicals after Keele. Keele led to Nottingham led to Caistor: all conferences which reflected the hope and growing confidence of the Evangelicals. But Keele was the watershed. The actual, realized ascendancy of the Evangelical party in the Church of England by the end of the century can be traced directly to the new openness and vitality emergent at Keele.

The third watershed date in the renewal of the Protestant profile in the Church of England was as much a fulfillment of the times as an anticipation of fresh successes. This was the 1991 appointment to Canterbury of Dr. George Carey. Carey, who came to his appointment by way of classic Anglican Evangelicalism — Dagenham parish church in Essex; Oak Hill Theological College; St. John's Theological College; Trinity College, Bristol: all stations on the way to his being appointed Bishop of Bath and Wells in 1987 — has, since his time at Lambeth began, distanced himself somewhat from the Evangelical world in which his ministry was early shaped. This is partly from the need for a comprehensive Christian vision, which the position of Canterbury requires. It is also partly from personal preference and his naturally *un*-conservative disposition. Dr. Carey has aspired not only to listen to Anglo-Catholics and Liberals in the Church, but actually to learn from them and take aboard some of their insights. His liberality of mind and his native open-mindedness, on many fronts, have resisted labeling. It is really true that when reporters have called him the "Evangelical Archbishop," he has sometimes peered at them uncomprehendingly. The advantage of this for the Church is a model of breadth *with* conviction that speaks well for the Church in an age of pluralism. A disadvantage, however, has been the coolness that many Evangelicals have come to feel from Carey since he became archbishop. Probably Carey will go down in history as an Archbishop of Canterbury who *came from* the definitely Evangelical tradition within the Church but who developed and possessed broad personal sympathies. From a church-historical point of view, however, his appointment will always be regarded as a high watermark of Evangelical credibility within the established Church of England.

The final summing up of this chapter relates to the present state of the Protestant profile in the Church of England. If by this we mean, as we necessarily have to mean since the forcing of Protestantism through the funnel of Evangelicalism as a result of the successes of Anglo-Catholicism in the late nineteenth century and as a result of the defeat by Protestant Anglican Evangelicals of the 1928 proposed Book, we must report that the present profile of Evangelicalism in the Church of England is well lit. It is in better repair than ever (since the Georgian-Hanoverian consensus in England so decisively measured by the Glorious Revolution of 1688). It threatens, in England at least, so to outshine the Catholic profile as almost to eclipse it.

Here it is absolutely fitting to underline the unique achievement of Anglican Evangelicals within the Church of England. The fact that they have remained *in the Church*, over more than two centuries, is something like a miracle. In almost every other national Protestant Church in Europe, Evangelicals have either been driven from the Church or seceded from it themselves. The "Pietists" of Württemberg in southwestern Germany are one of the very few other evangelical constituencies to have remained within the established Church of the region. And even there, and certainly in most of Germany, the distinction between "evangelisch" (recognized *bona-fide* Protestant "state-church" Christians) and "evangelikal" (conservative evangelicals scarcely recognized officially within the regular church structures) is a hard-and-fast one. This was, since Charles Simeon, and is, through the leadership of John Stott, not the case in England. The Evangelicals are at home in the Church of England. They are not always comfortable, and they have not always been "team players," but they "have a place at the table." Their voice is heard, and few in the Church are now able to stop their ears.

The Evangelical profile is also endangered, however, though not yet critically. A more "Catholic" critique would say that Anglican Evangelicalism is succumbing, as evangelicalism "always does," to fissiparousness. This is to say that in its very time of full bloom, it is threatening to split apart. That is true. There are presently "open Evangelicals," self-described as those clergy (they are mostly clergy) and laity who are open to the world, open to a change of mind regarding biblical interpretation and therefore the application of the Bible to questions like those concerning human sexuality, the rights of the dying, divorce, and abortion; open in general to the culture that surrounds the Church. Then there are "Reform" Evangelicals, who are conservative Evangelicals struggling for the Church as a whole to retain orthodox and traditional views on similar questions. The first group is comparable to the "liberal Evangelicals" of the 1920s and 1930s. The second group is comparable to the "conservative Evangelicals" who held the torch after 1928. There is at least a third group: the charismatic Evangelicals, springing from the Charismatic Renewal that swept the Church in the 1970s and now an enormous power in England by way of the London parish of Holy Trinity, Brompton, with its Anglican response to the "Toronto Blessing" of the 1990s. Pentecostalism has been mainly the province of Evangelical Church people in England, in contrast to its closer relation to broadly "catholic" circles in the American Church.

The three streams of Anglican Evangelicalism, "Open," "Reform," and "Charismatic," exist in some tension. This tension was evident at the National Evangelical Anglican Congress held at Caistor in 1988. It is even more evident today. Interestingly, the Reform group has resisted Carey's leadership as actively as any group within the Church of England, excepting the Traditionalist wing of the Anglo-Catholic party, who regard the Archbishop as a "Protestant Liberal."

So a more "Catholic" critique of the Evangelical party would point to the obvious divisions within Evangelical ranks as the fulfillment of Protestantism's inherent tendency towards individualism and subjectivism.

In fact, the pluralism of the Evangelical constituency inside the

Church of England is the result of its growth. Growth involves inclusion, and inclusion involves diversity of approach. An interesting question remains: Where is the Protestant interest within the Evangelical movement as it presently stands?

With the exception of the Reform group, Protestant self-consciousness is weak among the Evangelicals. It may, in fact, be stronger among "liberals" and "feminists" in the Church, who appeal to the free spirit of inquiry and progress unleashed by the Reformation protest. Authority and Protestantism have always existed in tension. And while the Reform Evangelicals cherish the Thirty-Nine Articles and the principal article, justification by grace through faith, they are uncomfortable with the intellectual freedom of the Enlightenment, even though that freedom was the natural child of the Reformation. Nevertheless, theologically speaking and proportionally speaking, the Reform element thinks of itself as consciously Protestant. David Watson's speech at Nottingham in 1977, in which he referred to the Reformation as possibly the greatest tragedy ever to befall Christendom, heralded an ecumenical spirit among the charismatic Evangelicals, whose he was, which has lessened the Protestant profile of *that* group. And the "Open Evangelicals" are uncomfortable with Protestantism in any sense in which it is associated with biblicism or doctrinal authority as such.

What then is the Protestant profile of the Church of England at the turning of the century? It is the Evangelical profile, to the extent that the Evangelicals will claim it. In one sense, the Protestant profile is strong. Historic Protestant emphases on the Word, and therefore also on the Bible; on personal faith as the root transaction of Christianity from our (i.e. humanity's) side; on the cross and resurrection as central and objective facts; on the importance of doctrine and therefore of orthodoxy; on the presence and action of God within the here and now: all these emphases remain strong among Anglican Evangelicals.

In another sense, the Protestant profile is weak. The word itself, *Protestant*, is seldom heard. The Reformation is little studied — more assumed than engaged. So important is bridge-building to the world as preparatory to evangelism and mission, that historic identity questions, except among members of the Reform group, do not come to the fore. Also, the note of protest sounded by the Reformation, the almost inherently anti-authority dimension within Protestant consciousness, is not often sounded among Evangelicals. Moreover, the intellectually *critical* side of the phenomenon, the Enlightenment side, we might say, is approached only with considerable caution by Evangelicals. The assumption, rather, that we exist within a post-modern age, an age in which Enlightenment critical reason no longer obtains or has meaning, has become an assumption widely held among Evangelicals. Therefore, the Enlightenment as *child of the Reformation* comes as an almost entirely new idea to those who are accustomed to think *negatively* of scientific criticism.

So, although one might think of the very full profile of Evangelicalism in the Church of England as being almost synonymous with the profile of Protestantism there, that would only be half true. Where are the protesting insights of Protestantism, its critical, urgently questioning method? *Perhaps* among the feminist theologians, who nevertheless see people like Luther and Calvin, not to mention Cranmer and Hooper, as overly systematic, male, and biblicist. *Perhaps* among the theologians of the relation of science and religion, who nevertheless are far more *process*-oriented in their thinking than the Reformers were who spoke of the "one, full, perfect and sufficient sacrifice." *Perhaps* among the theologians of political liberation, whose present mentors, however, are more often Roman Catholics of the southern hemisphere. *Perhaps* among the proponents of gay consciousness and gay rights and issues, although very few of these would seek for models among the Reformation figures, who made such an issue out of clerical marriage and who seem in their personae, with their consciously long beards and controversial wives, the very image of heterosexuality. Each of these alternative insights and groups carries elements of what Paul Tillich called "the Protestant Principle." They are working against the "powers that be," shaking the tree of received authority and received assumption. Each of these groups has *also*, however, not been accustomed to seeking its *fons originalis* in the sixteenth century. So we observe important aspects of Protestantism in all of them, but in every case the links are implicit.

It may be up to a still unheard *critical* voice within the ranks of the Anglican Evangelicals to shine a light on the Protestant profile, a profile that is very much there, beneath the Evangelical profile, but would almost always threaten to break forth from within it, loosening sections of the plaster and causing them to fall in pieces to the ground. The profile will be strongest, and hopefully most appealing and compelling to the rest of the world, when the theology of Protestantism is shown to cohere with its free, investigative method. That would be a truly fresh look on Christianity, something with which to surprise the world in the twenty-first century.

CHAPTER 4

The Protestant Face of Anglicanism in the American Episcopal Church (1607 to 1979)

The Protestant face of Anglicanism in the United States at one time had a very high profile. Protestant Evangelicals before the American Civil War were close to being the dominant force within the Episcopal Church. Protestant "low churchmanship" was in some respects, such as the retention of Morning Prayer as the principal Sunday service, more established for a longer period of time into our era and with wider geographical representation than was the case comparably in England. It is all the more striking, truly startling, in fact, that Protestant churchmanship has died back since 1979 to absolute ground zero.

Definite Protestant Christians within the Episcopal Church today are an indefinably small minority. The vast majority of charismatics, with whom prospective Protestants would have much in common, are Catholic in churchmanship and by general self-definition. And the few Evangelicals, fortified within a half-dozen fortress institutions, are seldom high on Protestantism as such, because of its associations with liberalism, and also because "evangelical" is derogation enough without another term being added that requires explanation. Protestant consciousness within ECUSA, which used to be called *PECUSA* (i.e., the Protestant Episcopal Church in the U.S.A.) is moribund. It was not ever so. I am arguing here that a restoration of Protestant identity in the Church is important for the future. It could span the gap between liberals and evangelicals, and also other conservative church people, because it unites intellectual freedom with the historic gospel.

I. A Church Unquestionably Protestant (1607-1776)

The first Anglican service held in the American colonies was read on April 26, 1607, by the Rev. Robert Hunt in Captain John Smith's settlement at Jamestown. The first Church of England colonists brought with them a Jacobean form of Anglicanism that reflected entirely the aspirations of those late Elizabethan Christians who just one generation earlier had regarded Counter-Reformation Spain as the Antichrist. John Smith and the colonists at Jamestown held the same views concerning Protestant Fortress England as had Sir Francis Drake.

Although considerable high churchmanship existed among colonial Episcopalians before the American Revolution — the classic example being Commissary Alexander Garden in Charleston, South Carolina, who proved extremely hostile to evangelicals in general and to George Whitefield in particular — no Anglican in the thirteen colonies would have understood the Church as anything other than a Protestant Church. There are no cases on record of Puritan Anglican clergy in the colonies. The late-Reformation ethos of an Archbishop Abbott or a Bishop Joseph Hall would not have existed in a world where the principle of *separation* from the Church was embodied in an actual geographical alternative in Massachusetts and Rhode Island. Nevertheless, the colonial Anglican Church was Protestant and stood solid with English efforts to resist Catholic French expansion into the New World. In a sense, like Queen Elizabeth who *had* to be a Protestant because of the conditions of her birth, the early English "official" settlers, in New York, Virginia, and the Carolinas, *had* to be Protestants because of the physical pressure of advancing French and Spanish and by definition Catholic competitors for the same territory.

The Evangelical Anglicans who after the American Revolution became the heirs of the Protestant tradition were nonexistent before independence. Evangelical preachers like Joseph Pilmore and the Wesleys themselves were regarded as Nonconformists, on the boundary between "Church" and "chapel." The single and remarkable exception on record is the Rev. Devereux Jarratt, minister of Bath Parish, Dinwiddie County, Virginia, from 1763 to 1801. Jarratt remained a generally ordered and native-born colonial Anglican minister. But his evangelical zeal contributed to revival in Virginia. Most of his followers became Methodists. He himself died in some despair concerning the spiritual torpor and pitiful statistics of numerical decline characterizing the Church of England in Virginia at the onset of the Revolution.

II. "This Sickness Is Not unto Death": The Weakened Protestant Church of the Early Republic (1776-1811)

The facts regarding the *formal* or institutional resuscitation of the Anglican Church in the U.S. after independence are well known. The formal resuscitation of the Church included the first General Convention in Philadelphia in 1789; the consecration of Samuel Seabury at Aberdeen, Scotland, as the first American Episcopal bishop; the ratification of the English Prayer Book for use in the new republic with only minor revisions, most importantly the "Scottish-Episcopal" Prayer of Consecration at the Communion; and the formal link between the English Church and the new Church as expressed in the notable preface to the 1793 Book:

> this Church is far from intending to depart from the Church of England in any essential point of doctrine, discipline, or worship; further than circumstances require.

The formal resuscitation of what had been the Church of England

61

in the colonies, however, was no guarantee of its *material* resuscitation. Viewed from the ground up, the church was in a pathetic condition. Rural Virginia and Maryland, for example, were dotted with old brick churches dating from the late seventeenth and early eighteenth centuries. They stood empty. To the mind of the majority of Americans, these church buildings symbolized England and the autocracy of king and prelate. This was true even in traditional planters' regions such as the "low country" of coastal South Carolina and the "tidewater" of southeastern Virginia.

Despite the formal charters of the Church and the preservation through Seabury of the form of episcopal succession, the Protestant Episcopal Church in the United States of America showed no signs of resurgence, at least from the outside. Jarratt's dismal report of the Virginia diocesan convention immediately following the revolution is matched by Bishop James Madison's depressed decision to retire, without retiring, from his duties as president of William and Mary College at Williamsburg.

The Protestant principle of *being* something rather than *appearing to be* something could only stand as the most painful criticism of American Episcopal life at the end of the century and in the first years of the new.

III. The Evangelical Awakening within the Church and the Protestant Expansion (1811-1873)

It is practical to date the material revival of Anglicanism in America from the ordination of William Meade at Williamsburg on February 24, 1811. Meade's mother had kept the faith during the darkest years, the years immediately following the Revolution, maintaining regular family prayers from the Book of Common Prayer and reading through the King James Bible. The infusion of a little Presbyterian influence helped Meade to grasp the great issue of justification by faith. Soon after his ordination began a ministry that almost single-handedly restored the spiritual vigor of the Church in Virginia. The story is told succinctly and extremely well by David Holmes in his essay "The Decline and Revival of the Church of Virginia."[1] It is told with special reference to the parallel career of Charles Petit McIlvaine, the second bishop of Ohio, in Diana H. Butler's *Standing in the Whirlwind*.[2] But it is told at its best in the out-of-print classic, *Men and Movements of the American Episcopal Church*, by E. Clowes Chorley (New York, 1948). This last book has never been equaled for its sympathetic description of the Evangelical awakening within the Church, partly because Chorley himself was a living successor of the events and characters he described.

The Evangelical Awakening in the Episcopal Church was exactly coincident with a rise in specifically Protestant consciousness in the Church. The earliest writings we have of the first Virginia and Maryland Evangelicals come from their journal *The Washington Theological Repertory*, a venture edited by about a dozen Episcopal clergy who served parishes in the area around the American Capital, mainly Georgetown, Alexandria, Southern Maryland, and Baltimore. These definite and self-identified Evangelicals were definite and self-identified Protestants. Here are some samples and quotes from the *Repertory* magazine:

> The principles upon which (the magazine) will be conducted are those of the Bible, as illustrated in the Articles, Liturgy, and Homilies of the Protestant Episcopal Church.
>
> If by Calvinism be meant the doctrine of original sin, sanctification by the Holy Spirit and justification by the sole merits of our Saviour Jesus Christ, we plead guilty to the charge. . . .
>
> Our plan is to humble the Sinner, and to exalt the Saviour; to show him the utmost depth of his depravity as the best and the only means of inducing him to fly for refuge to the Lord Jesus Christ.[3]

1. David Holmes, "The Decline and Revival of the Church of Virginia," in *Up from Independence* (Orange, Va., 1976), pp. 45-101.

2. Diana H. Butler, *Standing in the Whirlwind: Evangelical Episcopalians in Nineteenth-Century America* (Oxford, 1995).

3. Quotations from *The Washington Theological Repertory* as given in Butler, pp. 29ff.

A factor in the polemical cutting edge of the early American Evangelical/Protestant Anglicans was the active resistance to their style of worship and preaching on the part of Bishop Kemp of Maryland. Because these clergy, a true band of brothers, combined a high-profile Protestantism with a high-profile evangelicalism, they cherished soul-winning as much as they treasured historical theology. This meant that they emphasized the sermon over everything else in the liturgy. It also meant that they used the Prayer Book to win their hearers. The Book was not an end in itself. Rather, it was an effective means to an end.

A *locus classicus* for Protestant Anglican Evangelicalism in the early years of the nineteenth century is found in the following account, cited from Chorley, of one Sunday's preaching program by the Rev. Richard Channing Moore. The incident occurred when Moore was rector of St. Stephen's Church, New York City:

> A striking illustration of his power has been preserved. At the close of a Sunday afternoon service a member of the congregation rose and said, "Dr. Moore, the people are not disposed to go home; please give us another sermon." He complied. Still they remained hungry for the Word of life. A third sermon followed at the close of which the preacher said: "My beloved people, you must now disperse — for, although I delight to proclaim the glad tidings of salvation, my strength is exhausted, and I can say no more." As a result of that service sixty communicants were added to the parish.[4]

Such a degree of sincerity and consecration, paralleled by disinterested pastoral care, was instanced in dozens of cases by the early and also the second-generation Episcopal Evangelicals. By 1850 they had brought the Episcopal Church in Virginia to such a point of interest and participation that it was the leading body of Christians there before the Civil War. By 1850 they had created Evangelical dioceses

4. E. Clowes Chorley, *Men and Movements of the American Episcopal Church* (New York, 1948), p. 40.

also in Massachusetts, Delaware, Pennsylvania, Rhode Island, Ohio, and even Kansas, Kentucky, and Iowa. There were also important Evangelical parishes in New York City. Moreover, the Evangelicals had founded theological seminaries in Alexandria and Gambier, Ohio, with Philadelphia and Boston to follow.

When the influence of the Oxford Tractarian Movement began to be felt in America, it was resisted by the Evangelicals, who discerned it as a threat to the future of the Church somewhat earlier than most English Evangelicals did. The result of the Americans' vigorous controversy against the "Romanizing" trend imported from Oxford was twofold: (1) It made heroes of the early American ritualists who could believe they were pulling off something that was really "over the top"; and (2) it hardened the edges of Protestant churchmanship among the Evangelicals, creating a low-church identity that became quite radical over time.

The American phenomenon of religious fissiparousness broke out in 1873, when a small group of Episcopal Evangelicals, alarmed by the persecution of one of their own by Bishop Whitehouse of Chicago over rubrical omissions related to the service of Baptism, gathered together to consider leaving the Church. Led by Assistant Bishop Cummins of Kentucky, this small yet influential group of low churchmen became agitated enough to disregard the pleas of the still powerful Evangelical diocesan bishops. They seceded on December 2, 1873.

Although at the time the "Cummins schism," as it was known, and the Reformed Episcopal Church, as it came to be known, seemed a not overly subscribed split, it symbolized and in fact was the end of something important. It was the end of the marriage of Protestant Anglicanism with American Evangelicalism that had achieved so much for the Church over sixty years.

What could the old Evangelicals who *stayed* with the Church do to try to restore the old alliance? Very little, it turned out. Declining giants like Stephen Higginson Tyng Sr., Rector of St. George's Church, Manhattan, and Alfred Lee, the Bishop of Delaware, lambasted their former coreligionists and wept for the good old days. But the tide had turned. The more Protestant elements in the Church were attracted to "liberalism." Their Reformation legacy of intellectual freedom made the immediate descendants of the "once-married" (i.e., Evangelical/Protestant/Anglicans) into the broad-church liberals of the next two generations. The new turning, which coincided remarkably with the departure of the Reformed Episcopalians, was signaled by the highly public career of Phillips Brooks, who became the Bishop of Massachusetts in 1891, succeeding the Protestant Anglican Evangelical Manton Eastburn. No more Protestant figure has ever served as a diocesan bishop in the Episcopal Church than Phillips Brooks, but he loosened the once strong bond between Evangelical theology and Protestant churchmanship. What Brooks came to was Protestant churchmanship (witness the interior of Trinity Church, Copley Square, Boston as Brooks designed it with H. H. Richardson) in union with broadly orthodox yet knowingly liberal interpretations of the Bible.

IV. The Protestants Lose Their Evangelicalism (1873-1928)

In 1872 John Henry Hopkins Jr. declared that "the old Evangelical party is dead, dead, dead." Hopkins spoke prematurely but accurately. The younger Evangelicals had either left as part of the Cummins schism or metamorphosed into "broad churchmen." The older Evangelicals, who were mostly bishops or cardinal rectors on the edge of retirement, bemoaned the state of affairs. Their memoirs can be read in the dusty archival sections of the older Episcopal seminary libraries. Their funeral sermons were bound in leather, final testimony to their far-outdated zeal. And they were laid to rest. Who today has heard of William Bacon Stevens, Bishop of Pennsylvania; Henry Lee, Bishop of Iowa; Thomas Vail, Bishop of Kansas; Gregory Thurston Bedell, Bishop of Ohio; and Ozi W. Whitaker, Bishop of Nevada?

The Evangelicals died out rapidly after 1873, and broad churchmen replaced them. These were Protestants in respect to intellectual freedom but only minimally Protestant in respect to atonement and Christology. The Anglo-Catholics, militant and strongly gathered in the upper Middle West, grabbed the glamor. The future of the Episcopal Church lay in the amalgam "liberal Anglo-Catholicism."

The important historic difference with similar developments in England, which were normally watched with interest, even rapacity, and the urge to replicate, from the United States, was the lack in the American Church of a *patronage system*. The Church of England never did away with the historical circumstance according to which vicars and rectors were appointed by individuals, trusts, Oxbridge Colleges, and a whole complex network of institutions and even private persons who "owned the living." This patronage system, which sounds undemocratic to American ears, was crucial to the survival of the Evangelicals in the Church of England. Evangelical laymen and clergy purchased with foresight numbers of these livings in the first decades of the nineteenth century. They provided for an Evangelical succession, by will and testimony, in a considerable number of English "town" parishes. Thus positions were held vacant for Evangelical candidates "world without end" — to this day. An Evangelical constituency was created which was positioned to withstand the tides of theological fashion. The patronage system saved the Evangelical emphasis for the Church of England.

American Episcopalians, because of a totally different history arising from the Revolution of 1776, never even thought in such terms. They therefore had no bulwark to withstand the *Zeitgeist*. So they folded up. Only at Virginia Seminary, due mainly to the honoring of history and tradition for its own sake, did an Evangelical Protestant consciousness linger. But it was, again, more Protestant in *method* than in *theology*.

In 1928 a slightly revised Prayer Book was adopted by the Protestant Episcopal Church in the United States of America. This signaled a period of stability and a relative lack of controversy in the Church that persisted almost four decades.

V. Protestant = "Liberal Evangelical" = Morning Prayer Parish (1928-1979)

This digest of American Episcopal history does not treat the tumultuous decade of the 1960s, tumultuous in relation to the Civil Rights struggle, the Vietnam war, and the other controversies of that decade. It does simply say that Protestantism for PECUSA was a weakened entity, more implicit than explicit, carried by the so-called "liberal Evangelicals" such as Alexander Zabriskie, Walter Russell Bowie, and Angus Dun. It was modeled within the multitude, still the dominant number until 1979, of traditional Episcopal parishes that offered Morning Prayer as the principal service on three Sundays of the month. All this changed, very rapidly and in the longer view, overnight, after 1979.

The writer grew up in the light of liberal Evangelicalism as represented not so long ago by the Dioceses of Washington and Virginia, grown quite parallel around the Potomac River. I grew up reading Dr. Bowie on the Bible and Church History and listening to Bishop Dun in the pulpit. Protestantism was assumed, if seldom stated. Liberalism had a benign open-mindedness, and the sharper edge of polemical radicalism in theology existed, but way out in San Francisco — Bishop Pike, in short. The link of Protestant liberalism with evangelicalism, however, was unacknowledged, save in Bowie's regard for the Reformation and in his celebrated allergy to Bishop Manning of New York's militant doctrinaire Anglo-Catholicism.

An important result, however, of the revolutionary 1960s was the Trojan Horse of the 1979 Book of Common Prayer.

VI. Protestantism as an Empty Set (1979-)

The zeal for revolutionary change that marked the culture of the late 1960s and early 1970s extended to a zeal for liturgical change. New orders for liturgy seemed part of the package for a revolutionary Church. So a Prayer Book alternative seemed a natural evolution, or rather development.

The irony, however, is that those who proved most interested in liturgy and who became the authors of the new Book had little tolerance for the *theology* of the old Book. Moreover, they were catholicizers on the surface, while remaining 1960s rebels at deeper levels. We know now that the architects of the 1979 Book were uncomfortable with the penitential tone of the old Communion service, even in its Scottish form which Samuel Seabury had bargained for. They also took the line that the Communion service was the *only* authentic principal service for a Christian Church. Therefore they tailored the Book entirely around the "Eucharist," as it now became known, and they softened wherever possible the themes of repentance and atonement.

The 1979 Prayer Book was therefore a Trojan Horse, carrying within a framework of change-for-change's-sake the stealthy germs of anti-Reformation emphasis and the very un-Protestant notion that it would *supplant* rather than enhance the existing Book. The whole episode, which is very much with us still, was the oddest constellation of revolution, autocracy, and surface "catholicism." What we are left with now is amnesia regarding what once was; a negative judgment placed on any service but the so-called Rite II Holy Eucharist; and a false smile of "celebration," like the Cheshire Cat's, which covers over the mystery and tragedy of human pain. With the approval and lightning ascent of the 1979 Prayer Book came the end, for all practical purposes, of Protestant churchmanship in what is now known aggressively as ECUSA.

Will the Protestant face of Anglicanism in the American Episcopal Church ever be restored? One looks to England, where it remains quite strong. One looks to sections of the worldwide Anglican Communion that may in themselves be strong enough culturally to resist somewhat the American hegemony. One reads the Articles daily and holds close to the Bible. One reads history, although *that* can become romanticism rather than contemporary fuel for the gospel fire. One prays the ancient response: "And take not thy Holy Spirit from us."

CHAPTER 5

The Face Restored

"And we all, with unveiled face, beholding the glory of the Lord, are being changed into his likeness from one degree of glory to another."

2 CORINTHIANS 3:18

For the renewal of Anglicanism to take place, it is required that a renewal of Christianity within Anglicanism take place. What is *not* required is a renewal of "Anglicanism" defined as some *tertium quid* which carries special value in itself. Such a view of "renewal" is seen in an exchange not so long ago at an American Episcopal clergy conference. One rector affirmed, "We sure need to rediscover the importance of evangelism!" Another commented, "Yes, we need to know more about our Anglican identity so we can know what we are really sharing." This second, "clarifying" comment bespoke disaster and a worrisome confusion. The comment implied that the Church has this quantity, "Anglicanism," the manna of which the world is dying to partake. Such a view, not to mention its sectarian understanding of Church, totally underestimates the gravity of the human situation, the depth of pain to which the world religions speak, and the particular radicality of God's engagement with sin, death, and the law which Christianity affirms. If it is Anglicanism

71

as a blessed *tertium quid* that is "such as we have to give" (Acts 3:6), then we are "of all men most to be pitied" (1 Cor. 15:19)!

What is required in view of the enduring pain of the world is the renewal of *Christianity* within Anglicanism. This does not trample on Anglican distinctives. But it views them in proportion to the deeper concerns for which this Church has been the bearer in certain times and places, in particular within the English-speaking Reformation legacy known as the Church of England, together with its daughter churches.

For Christianity itself to be renewed within Anglicanism, the Protestant profile of the Church requires restoration. The Reformation carried certain emphases and highlights that are essential in order for the Christian gospel to arrest the attention of the world. The Catholic insights have had their day in the sun, nor is their day done. But the Protestant insights offer a vital element. Without their restoration, the Anglican Church will fall short of its potential to carry the flame of God's Word into the next generation. We shall be supplanted, if not confined, like C. S. Lewis's denizens of hell, to our isolated individual spaces, increasingly detached from the clamoring world which pleads so unstoppably for deliverance.

The first step in restoring the Protestant face of Anglicanism, which may in our time be equivalent to the restoration of Christianity itself within Anglicanism, is to affirm a Protestant-Anglican understanding of salvation.

A. A Protestant-Anglican Christology

Christology is the teaching concerning Jesus Christ. It is the teaching concerning the identity of Christ: Who was he? What did he do? *Atonement* refers to what Jesus Christ achieved, specifically to what he achieved in his death. And *justification by grace through faith* refers to the benefits that accrue to the human race, and to individual human beings concretely, by *virtue* of Christ's atonement. It is a three-part progression, the sum of which constitutes salvation, or deliverance. Jesus Christ was, Jesus Christ did, and Jesus Christ gives.

That which makes a Christology *Protestant* is the central emphasis placed on it within the framework of Christian theology as the *single most important thing* (*solus Christus* or "Christ alone" in the parlance of the Reformers). That which makes a Christology also Anglican is the continuity of its *primacy*, or supreme emphasis, within the charter documents and founding insights of the Church of England. There is no uniquely *Anglican* Christology, nothing more or less unique than the central place given it in all Christian confessions, of which the Thirty-Nine Articles is one. Nevertheless, we are fortunate within our tradition to have the Articles, which affirm a fully developed and clearly stated Protestant Christology.

The threefold progression of our Christology is fundamental. To spotlight this cornerstone of Protestant Anglicanism we can frame it in the form of three theses.

> THESIS ONE The Son, which is the Word of the Father, begotten from everlasting of the Father, the very and eternal God, and of one substance with the Father, took man's nature in the womb of the blessed Virgin, of her substance: so that two whole and perfect natures, that is to say, the Godhead and Manhood, were joined together in one Person, never to be divided, whereof is one Christ, very God, and very Man. (Article II)

This statement of classic Christology is the formal teaching of the Anglican Church concerning Jesus Christ, the full expression in the flesh of God. There is nothing peculiar to Protestantism in this truly lapidary statement of faith, nor anything peculiar to Anglicanism as such. On the other hand, it links us with the classic statements of all the Christian churches concerning the uniqueness of Christ's fully human (i.e., historical) and fully divine (i.e., outside of history) natures. It is *Thesis One* of a Protestant-Anglican Christology because it is the starting point. We do not start with a theology of creation. The idea that God or a god created the world may be considered a surmise, even a conclusion, based upon observation and human reason, but it is not the starting point of Christianity. The starting point of Christianity is more specific and less abstract. God became "one of us." This is the essence and starting point of Christianity.

We can say without apology that Protestant-Anglicanism indicates a theology *from the ground up.* This is to say, we begin with the Christ who came into the world. Our starting point is the event in time, in the remote and fractious Roman province of Palestine, outside of which our knowledge of God would be speculative. Thus Protestant Anglicanism is skeptical concerning "natural theology" as it is usually invoked. Natural theology is the notion that we can induce attributes of deity from the creation, that is, from nature itself, without necessary reference to revelation, in particular without necessary reference to the particularity of Jesus of Nazareth.

We say, rather, that the God revealed by nature, "in whom we live and move and have our being" (Acts 17:28; St. Paul is quoting from the Greek philosopher Epimenides), is an enigma. For every characteristic of harmony and beauty which we can induce from the world's order, we can match characteristics such as caprice, lethal disaster, and pitilessness. The world on its own terms is no canvass for a portrait of God that is either unified or compassionate. (The world's picture of God, based on sorry experience, might more closely resemble the Picture of Dorian Gray!) Natural theology is speculative. We therefore choose a theology from the ground up, not in the *recent* sense of a theology based on experience in general terms, or based on human insight as its starting point; but from the ground up in the sense of the historic starting point for all knowledge of God being in "the face of Christ" (2 Cor. 4:6). Our theology begins, for lack of any other solid platform, from the claim of the historical enfleshment of deity within history. Thus Article II of the Thirty-Nine Articles of Religion.

> **THESIS TWO** The offering of Christ once made is that perfect redemption, propitiation, and satisfaction, for all the sins of the whole world, both original and actual; and there is none other satisfaction for sin, but that alone."

This is a portion of the Thirty-First Article of Religion, entitled "Of the one Oblation of Christ finished upon the Cross." It is the crucial *interpretation* of the historical report, which constitutes our theology from the ground up, for it "theologizes" solely on the basis of a recorded instance of particular history. This article interprets the cross. Emphasized here is the perfectness of the sacrifice of Christ, as being an achievement by which the penalty and burden of all human sin were canceled and taken away. The article features classic language of medieval theology (words such as "redemption," "propitiation," and "satisfaction") in the service of attributing to Christ's cross an achievement that cannot be added to or subtracted from.

This article is specifically *Protestant* in two respects: (1) it eliminates the notion of the Mass as a continuing sacrifice for sin, placing the *entire weight* of salvation on the one thing done "once for all" (see the Prayer of Consecration in the Prayer Book of 1549 through Rite I of 1979); (2) it affirms the scope and coverage of Christ's historic achievement to include *both* the "original" or inherent intrinsic sin within all human beings *and* specific or actual sins committed. The article covers both the *state* of the human race and the *actions* of the race. The past, in other words, relates efficaciously both to the psychogenetic legacy of a man (original sin) and the works (actual sins) of a man, and all of them. Catholicism had understood that every sin committed in life needed specific expiation, to be accomplished on a specific continuing basis through regular confession and the hearing of Mass. Protestantism discerned the acute *insecurity* of such an understanding. Every time you sinned, you had to go to Confession and then to Mass in order to be forgiven. Protestantism saw this pattern as a derogation from the finality of Christ's achievement and also as the endangerment of any one person's full assurance of forgiveness. Forgiveness seemed, on the Catholic model, to be conditional on a person's application to a priest for specific remission in respect to a specific sin. That model, on the Reformers' view, opened the whole issue of forgiveness of sin to casuistry, which is the science of measuring individual guilt against a quantified hierarchy of satisfactions for guilt. At one stroke the Reformers abolished the uncertain character of forgiveness. They placed the whole weight on the "perfect redemption, propitiation, and satisfaction" of Christ (Article XXXI).

Thus Protestant-Anglican Christology, having started with the enfleshment of God in the historic figure of Jesus, singles out the cross as the achievement par excellence of God in the salvation of men. Our Christology focuses on the particular, which is the cross. It is not content with the incarnation as such, the visitation of God to the world. That visitation is conceived of as having an end or goal. *The end* is the cross, and the empty tomb that follows. Thus the character of God as Pardoner becomes indelible.

How is this indelible character of God as Pardoner *grasped?* We can now proceed to the third component of the Protestant-Anglican Christology, justification by faith.

> THESIS THREE We are accounted righteousness be-
> fore God, only for the merit of our Lord and Saviour
> Jesus Christ by Faith, and not for our own works or
> deservings. Wherefore, that we are justified by Faith
> only, is a most wholesome Doctrine, and very full of
> comfort, as more largely is expressed in the Homily of
> Justification.[1]

This is the eleventh article of the Thirty-Nine. It identifies the cutting edge of Christology. It marks the spot where engagement takes place between the objective givenness of Christ's achievement and the erratic subjectivity of human experience.

Justification by faith is the cutting edge of Christology because it is the point of contact with the universal human aspiration for recognition. Everyone is seeking recognition. Recent decades have sometimes termed this the search for self-worth. At the end of the millennium we are more inclined to use the word *inclusion*, "having a place at the table." Every era employs its own vocabulary. Bible

---

1. The Homily of Justification, attributed to Thomas Cranmer, can be found in the 1986 reprint of *The Homilies* (Lewes, 1986), pp. 13-21; also in *English Reformers*, ed. T. H. L. Parker (Philadelphia, 1966), pp. 262-71.

language considers this universal human aspiration to be the quest for justification. I need, in Bible language, to be justified or pronounced righteous before God. Luther asked the question thus: "Wie kriege ich einen gnädigen Gott?" (How can I find a gracious God?) How can I gain God's positive recognition? How can I become legitimated — justified — in the sight of the *one* entity whose opinion matters?

The traditional answer to this question is, by means of *earning* my justification: by doing *everything* I am supposed to do, and doing it perfectly. The New Testament sees this traditional answer as completely inadequate. It is an answer that is full of holes. Human experience, let alone the *a priori* fact of God's perfection by definition, reveals the impossibility of achieving perfection. Human beings are unable, empirically, to justify themselves. The quest for satisfactory self-worth and full inclusion within the finished circle of unqualified acceptance cannot ever be completed. That is because of flawed human nature. Our human nature is constitutionally weakened. It cannot perform in such a way as to be recognized as perfect.

Thus Article XI of the Thirty-Nine Articles understands justification by faith to carry comfort. To put this in its precise theological form: We are justified by God's grace as expressed in the pardoning substitutionary death of Christ on the cross and this grace is received by trusting, or faith. God has justified us, something we are unable to do for ourselves. This justification from outside ourselves is for the receiving. The true heart of religion is trust in the gift of God.

Protestant-Anglican Christology, therefore, begins with the historical embodiment of the invisible enigmatic God in the man Jesus Christ of Nazareth. The end to which this embodiment tends is the sacrificial death of Christ, by which our sins become his and his sinlessness, or perfection, is ascribed to us. We are therefore justified, being now regarded as righteous, or sinless, or perfect, by virtue of the transfer of guilt. Trust, or faith in this new status, constitutes the only efficacious religious act in the world. Such trust bears no relation whatsoever to any intrinsic gifts/merits or flaws/debits that lie within our genes, our psyche, or within our past life experience. The whole issue of worth has been taken out of our hands. The point of Christology is to transfer from us to God the burden of the restless, chronic quest for recognition and acceptance.

B. A Protestant-Anglican Doctrine of Grace

The implications of one phrase from Article XI are important. They carry us forward to a Protestant-Anglican doctrine of grace. The phrase is this: "that we are justified by Faith only, is a most wholesome Doctrine, and very full of comfort." "Wholesome" and "very full of comfort": these are words of healing in the face of pain.

The Reformers saw the message of justification as a word of comfort, first and primarily, to the troubled conscience. The conscience, unable to convince itself of its worth, justification, or inclusion within the circle of satisfying acceptance, was understood and actually felt to be the burdened Achilles' heel of human consciousness in general. The conscience, then as now, was the point of maximum *stress* in the human situation. Luther had identified this exact point of stress in his breakthrough document of 1518, entitled "A Disputation Concerning the Investigation of Truth and the Comfort of Alarmed Consciences." Luther understood from the beginning of his reforming work that the universally experienced problem of perceived unworthiness, or guilt in the deepest sense, had to be the problem to which religion, in order to be any good to us, must address itself. At the cutting edge of Christology that is denominated by the words *justification by faith*, Luther discerned the true potential for "wholesomeness" and "comfort" incipient within Christianity. Everything beside that was *beside the point.* The word of Jesus Christ had to strike home here, in the conscience, for it to be credible — as opposed to a false promise, a pretty picture, an instructive story.

The English Reformers, as demonstrated officially in the Articles and Homilies of the Church of England, adopted Luther's insight concerning justification all across the line. William Tyndale's debt to this insight became the debt owed by all English Protestants. This debt developed into a doctrine of *grace* that is, we could fairly say, the subjective or practical, even the existential, flash point of Protestant Anglicanism.[2]

Justification by faith implies the positive imputation of Christ's perfection to us, and the corresponding *negative* imputation of our imperfections to him, in the moment of time demarked by his absolutely desolate death on the cross. This is the means of the transfer of guilt. The burden of our inwardly perceived and outwardly enacted, unpayable debt to stress — which is, religiously understood, the demand of God — is transferred, or imputed *away* from us. What we receive is the ascription or reckoning of Christ's perfection. The transfer is complete: an either/or transaction. We are regarded as completely righteous, and he is regarded, at that moment of abject forsakenness, as completely human.

Richard Hooker, the Church of England's apologist in respect to extreme Puritanism and also in respect to Roman Catholicism in the later years of Queen Elizabeth I, summed up the "wholesome," "comfortable" factor of imputation within his "Learned Treatise of Justification":

> The righteousness wherein we must be found, if we will be justified, is not our own; therefore we cannot be justified by any inherent quality. Christ hath merited righteousness for as many as are found in him. In him God findeth us, if we be faithful; for by faith we are incorporated into him. Then, although in ourselves we be altogether sinful and unrighteous, yet even the man which in himself is impious, full of iniquity, full of sin; him being found in Christ and through faith, and having his sin in hatred through repentance; him God beholdeth with a gracious eye, putteth away his sin by not imputing it, taketh quite away the punishment due thereunto, by pardoning it; and accepteth

2. For a full and very positive discussion of the *later* Anglican debt to Luther's insight, and in particular the great F. D. Maurice's debt, see Paul Avis, *Anglicanism and the Christian Church* (Minneapolis, 1989), pp. 239-70. Avis's review of the nineteenth-century reception of the Reformation by more liberal Anglican voices is unique in recent literature.

him in Jesus Christ, as perfectly righteous, as if he had fulfilled all that is commanded him in the law.[3]

Richard Hooker's account of imputation is definitive for the Protestant-Anglican doctrine of grace. It leads irresistibly to the sharpest edge of all, the teaching known as *simul iustus et peccator*, "at the same time justified and a sinner." In more contemporary language, we could say that this is the teaching according to which the human being who has been justified by grace through faith is simultaneously fully human and also perfectly beloved by God. Grace imputed to the human being creates the intrapsychic situation, the *felt* situation, in which we are unqualifiedly cherished and yet at the same time more aware than ever of our humanity, hence of our imperfections. The *either/or* of the full forgiveness of sin achieved on the cross results in the *both/and* of human experience as new creation. We are both fully new and terminally old, accepted and repentant, inflated by hope and ever deflated by our own self-knowledge. The situation becomes one of irrepressible confidence in God and the realistic measurement of our own weakness. *Hope* and *realism*, inextricably linked by the teaching of imputation, is the vantage point from which Christian experience is lived out.

The development, then, of a Protestant-Anglican theology of grace is not essentially different from the development of classic Reformation theology across the Protestant schools of thought and nations. The starting point is the historic incarnation of God. The end towards which the incarnation was conceived in the first place is the atoning death of Jesus, the substitutionary sacrifice for sin, the moment of guilt-transfer by which alone the human being can become justified. Justification results from the cross, from its transfer of guilt, and this justification is grasped subjectively by an act or attitude of trust. Justification is the transfer of guilt and perfection by means of the holy imputation. "For our sake he [God] made him [Christ] to be sin who knew no sin, so that in him we might become the righteousness of God" (2 Cor. 5:21). Imputation carries through

---

3. Richard Hooker, "A Learned Discourse of Justification," in *In the Laws of Ecclesiastical Polity I* (London, 1958), p. 21.

to the realization, quite counter to "normal" human thinking, that we are *simul iustus et peccator,* unfailingly loved and at the same time fully human. This is *the* liberating insight and applied subjective legacy of grace that has come about through the Christology of Protestantism, and in its historically mediated form in England, through the Christology of Protestant Anglicanism.

Protestant Anglicanism is, if it is anything, a theology of grace.

C. A Protestant-Anglican Concept of Intellectual Freedom

"Anglicanism," which as a term covers at least two fundamentally differing understandings of its own identity, the "Catholic" and the "Protestant," is typically seen as a religious construction that values reason. The way this is usually put is that our concept of authority puts *Scripture* first, whereby we accept as authoritative those truths concerning which Scripture speaks unequivocally or consistently. Where Scripture does not speak univocally, or where it does not speak at all (i.e., of the proper use of music in the church — a secondary matter — or of doctrines such as the Trinity — a primary matter), we submit our ideas to the authority of *tradition.* The tradition of the church has developed, as well as sometimes ruled out, understandings of God and Christ that are implicit in the Bible but not fully developed there; or applications of Christianity to situations that did not exist in Bible times. Tradition is the interpretation of Scripture over time, resulting in insights, some of them hopefully inspired by the Holy Spirit of God, that have endured and become of full membership in the Christian Church almost on a par with the unique historic revelation of the Bible itself. The third element or "leg" of the Anglican construction of authority is human *reason.* When we encounter questions that are resolved neither from the Bible nor from the tradition, questions such as those regarding quantum physics or automobile maintenance or nuclear fission, or even ethical propositions like cheap mass transit or the limitations of cloning, we submit our judgments to *reason.* Human reason can be used to establish and verify generalizable results.

Thus Anglicanism is identified by many of its proponents as resting on a "three-legged stool": Scripture, tradition, and reason, in that order of priority. With its authority, Scripture establishes many things, such as the incarnation, the atonement, and justification by faith. Tradition enhances Scripture by establishing other things, such as the proper interpretation/s of the Last Supper, the character of God as Triune, and the various possibilities for godly government of the Church. Reason enhances tradition and Scripture by thinking through *what is right to do now*, given changing conditions, evolving knowledge, and the results of scientific investigation.

The Protestant element within Anglicanism is that element which chiefly honors *reason* as the best enhancement to Scripture. The Protestant element within Anglicanism is less comfortable with tradition, partly because tradition persistently holds up the Christian Church as intermediating between Scripture and humanity, while Protestants believe no intermediary is necessary.

The Protestant value attached to reason is not a phenomenon of the Renaissance. It does not spring from or relate to the importance claimed for reason by Renaissance thinkers such as Erasmus of Rotterdam. The Protestant value attached to reason results from the observation that the gospel of grace does not exist in 100 percent correlation to *all* of Holy Scripture. Luther's breakthrough concerning justification led to the birth of biblical criticism, for he saw clearly that the overwhelmingly dominant message of the Bible concerning atonement and grace was nevertheless not the unanimous witness of the entire Scripture. Enough was known even in Luther's time regarding the evolution of the canon of the New Testament for him to be aware that some books in Scripture had been canonized later than others, that the Book of Revelation was very late, that James and 2 Peter were in some contrast, especially with respect to law and grace, to the letters of Paul, and that even portions of some Pauline letters were regarded (by Paul himself!) as matters of opinion rather than as the Word of the Lord. Luther's theology of grace, which was the cutting edge of his Christology, lit up some contrarieties in the Bible with which reason had to wrestle. Tradition had tended to minimize and even swallow whole these problems, reducing reason's role to the uncomfortable one of covering over, "rationalizing," or apologizing for insuperable problems within the text.

While the weight that Luther attached to reason was received more enduringly in his native country and language than it was received in England, the weight of reason in arguing from Scripture *against* church tradition was a principle firmly established from the earliest days of Protestantism *in England*.

In England, however, the main arena for the use of reason in the work of Reformation was the debate concerning the sacrament of Holy Communion. Cranmer and Ridley, for example, were highly consequent thinkers who slashed up and down the Catholic tradition of transubstantiation, arguing against it with massive learning and irrefragable logic. In England, the Protestant valuation of reason did not involve, as it did in Germany, the investigation of the gospel of grace in relation to the inconsistencies of some Scriptures on the theme, but rather centered on the dialogue or controversy between *Scripture* on the Lord's Supper and the *traditions of the Church*, aided somewhat by late medieval philosophy, regarding the Mass. To read Nicholas Ridley's *Treatise on Transubstantiation*[4] is to read the thrilling discoveries of a man who was using his head as he read the Bible!

Ever since the burnings at the stake of scholars like Ridley, Protestant Anglicanism has had an allergy to the absolutism of tradition. This extended a century later to the way the English people vomited out the absolutism of the High Church movement as engineered by William Laud. It is not recognized in many treatments of "Anglicanism" how truly *un*-Anglican Archbishop Laud was, especially in regard to his method. His method was torture, ejection, and exile of as many as possible of those who disagreed with him. I find no evidence of the use of reason in the man's work at all — save for the use of *reason as calculation* to the unworthy end of conspiracy. I believe we can lay the responsibility for the establishment of reason as one norm for authority at the door of the Protestant Reformers,

4. Nicholas Ridley, "A Treatise Against the Errour of Transubstantiation, and Extracts from His Examinations," in *English Reformers*, ed. Parker, pp. 298-320.

whose later legatees included William Chillingworth, Lucius Cary, and their circle in the seventeenth century; John Locke and Bishop Burnet; Archbishop Tilletson and his school of thought in the eighteenth century; and F. D. Maurice and his students in the nineteenth century. In our own century reason has been generally valued as a requirement and mark of true religion. The Protestant-Anglican tradition is irresistibly liberal in the value it places on reason.

Here, incidentally, Protestantism within Anglicanism exists in tension with conservative Evangelical elements within Anglicanism itself, the very Evangelical strand with which otherwise it holds very much in common. It should be stated here that the restoration of the Protestant face of Anglicanism will depend in part on the degree to which reason is once again esteemed as the second, not the third, of the historic three legs of authority. For the Protestant Anglican who seeks to live in succession to the Reformation, authority is derived first from the Bible, secondly from reason as applied to thinking our way through the Bible, and thirdly from tradition, which we honor, flawed as it is by historical accident and the caprice of context, yet nevertheless sometimes well tested by means of the simple passage of time.

Protestant-Anglicanism's gospel of grace is linked necessarily to intellectual freedom.

D. A Protestant-Anglican Understanding of Church

The English poet Sir John Betjeman made a lifelong study of English parish churches. He loved old churches of almost any vintage, and although he was more attracted to the "Anglo-Catholic" variety, he saw the whole picture of the Church of England with broad sympathy. His description of the parish churches of the county of Herefordshire contains a classic Betjeman sentence: "For its size there is more 17th Century woodwork and Georgian box-pewing in Herefordshire than elsewhere. The county seems to have gone straight from 'High Church' to Evangelical. . . . No county has a church so wonderful as Abbey Dore, that solemn Cistercian Early English abbey with its 17th-Century woodwork . . . and for unrestored remoteness there is little to compare with Clodock."[5]

Betjeman was right! The whole range of English church self-understanding can be found in one county. We can compare the two parish churches Betjeman has lifted up, Abbey Dore and Clodock, as a representative key to understanding the *affirmation* as well as the *negation* which constitutes a Protestant-Anglican understanding of church.[6]

The *negation* applies to Abbey Dore, which embodies an impulse that Protestantism rejects. In 1634 Sir John Scudamore restored the ruinous old abbey church in its (then as now) remote setting. But he restored it *ideologically*, in the manner of what is now called Laudian High Churchmanship. Specifically, he had installed a massive solid oak screen, designed by John Abel, a gifted local joiner, to separate the sanctuary, where the Communion service was celebrated by the priest, from the nave, where the lay congregation was. The governing principle was *sacred space*, the idea that the area consecrated to sacred use (i.e., the celebration of the Sacrament) should be set visibly apart from the rest of the church — the less sanctified areas — and from the unsanctified themselves, the nonpriests or parish congregation. The screen, though now installed further west than its original location, conveys the controlling idea. Separation of God from man and man from God. Abbey Dore church has, therefore, its English version of a "holy of holies." The God who is of purer eyes than to behold iniquity may be approached by the priest alone, who can then carry the consecrated bread and wine to the people, who are seated West of Sinai!

The Protestant principle within Anglicanism generally rejects this notion of sacred separation. "God is worshiped not on this mountain nor in Jerusalem but in spirit and in truth" (St. John 4:21, 23, 24). The tabernacle of God is with his people. As St. Paul writes, "Now

---

5. *Collins Pocket Guide to English Parish Churches: The North,* ed. John Betjeman (London, 1968), pp. 136-37.

6. These comments on Clodock and Abbey Dore are based on personal visits to both in 1987.

you are the Body of Christ, and individually members of it" (1 Cor. 12:27). Richard Hooker wrote in the later days of the Elizabethan Reformation that the "real presence of Christ's most blessed body and blood is not therefore to be sought for in this sacrament, but in the worthy receiver of the sacrament."[7]

Beautiful, exquisite as it is, the great wood screen of Abbey Dore church earths a principle of mediatedness and religious separation that runs counter to the affirmation of God's grace as unmediated save through the Spirit of Christ and therefore not confined to a space.

At this point an objection is sometimes raised. It is objected that a God who is by definition in all places is by specification in no place! If we eschew the principle of God's locatedness in the sacrament or in the sacred meeting place and appointed time, then we locate God nowhere, or at least only invisibly — which to the average person makes God unattainable and hidden. There is a truth to this objection. The truth is that human beings need a *place* to meet with God. We are just so made that we require the outward and visible sign.

It is a striking fact that in a Reformed environment like the northwest cantons of Switzerland, where the churches since the Reformation have not been regarded as sacred space but rather as meeting houses and as an extension of the state, it is not customary for people to visit the churches midweek, or at any time other than 11 o'clock Sunday morning. Therefore the churches are locked. Always! If you wish to pray or just be quietly alone with your thoughts before God, you have to find a Roman Catholic church. I remember praying, during a difficult time personally, at a Lourdes-Grotto in Zürich, simply because it was the only church (shrine!) in walking distance that was open. I would have preferred the clear glass and restrained woodwork of a Protestant church. One took what one could get!

We can see why the Protestant tradition has been accused of being a secularizing trend, even an instrument of secularization.

---

7. As quoted in Stephen Neill, *Anglicanism*, 4th ed. (Oxford and New York, 1977), p. 124.

Certainly in Europe the historic Protestant countries *feel* more secular than the historically Catholic ones.

Yet the Protestant principle in its ideality retains its appeal and importance. If the spark of Christian conversion is lit, the flame burns from the sense of God and man joined, personally, in the here and now, no curtain between them save that of our sins. And these are forgiven in the here and now, without regard to their enormity or their number. The relief of pardon is the relief of unmediated converse and acceptance on the part of a hitherto hidden and enigmatic but now revealed God.

So we criticize the principle behind Abbey Dore's interior appointments, even as we admit that the Protestant criticism of "sacred space," if and when separated from its conversion-root, is consistent with religionlessness and aridity.

A few miles from Abbey Dore is the isolated church of Clodock. It is hard even to glimpse from the road, which is a one-lane track, and is overhung by a fairly threatening view of the dark Welsh hills known as the Black Mountains. The aisleless stone church is nevertheless a moving evocation and affirmation of the Protestant-Anglican experience of church.

The church is ancient in foundation, dedicated to the little known early saint Clydog. In the late 1600s, perhaps thirty years after John Scudamore imposed his wooden screen at Abbey Dore, Clodock parish church was fitted for Prayer-Book worship. The pulpit is three-decker and dominates the whole space. The altar is a table, beautifully carved but by no means as compelling as the pulpit. The box pews are all oriented to the pulpit, as is the west gallery. The windows in the church are clear glass. The entire scene has a sublime purity, yet with the highest quality of material and craftsmanship. This is an auditory church, yet in continuity with the founding Celtic saint himself. We could accurately describe this building as a defining moment for the Protestant yet native and continuous Church of England.

To travel from Abbey Dore to Clodock, recognizing the comparative grandeur and aesthetic weight of the former's sacred space, is nevertheless to travel from Samaria and Jerusalem (St. John 4:20) to the unmediated religion (4:23-24) of Jesus.

A Protestant-Anglican experience of Church is one of ideality. It is an experience of the nonmediated grace of God. This experience is heartfelt and personal, and also highly supportive of the *people* as the dwelling place of God. We are the tabernacle of the Spirit. The geography goes this way: The Word of God is first heard by the preacher as the vertical communication of revelation. This Word, engaging the hearer in the form of the cardinal affirmation of God's justification of the ungodly and unworthy, travels from the preacher to the people. Individually and by extension collectively, the people are made the Body of Christ on earth. This is the church. Thus we are unapologetic about auditory churches of grace. Sacrament is Word made manifest. The governing concept is nonmediation, or, positively said, direct encounter.

An old Episcopal church had carved over its quite elaborate marble altar the words, "He is not here." A country chapel not far away had lettered on its Easter Day outdoor notice-board the words, "He is not here." Both of these messages were not finished. What they *meant* to say was, "He is not here, for he is risen" (St. Matt. 28:6). He is not limited to geographical space, for he is everywhere. Chief of all, he is in our lives by faith, impelling, motivating, loving, reassuring, creating fresh confidence. This is also the Protestant-Anglican experience of church: he is not here (he is everywhere — and with you and me in particular and specifically), for he is risen.

Seventy years ago a great old Evangelical and very Protestant clergyman of the Church of England called Daniel Bartlett was amicably chided by the then Archbishop of Canterbury: "What does it feel like, Bartlett, out there, right out there, on the extreme end?" "No, Your Grace," retorted Bartlett, flashing his impish, mouselike smile, "Not at the extreme. I'm right at the heart, the very center of Christianity."[8]

---

8. The story is told by Michael Saward in his *Evangelicals on the Move* (London and Oxford, 1987), p. 91.

Selected Reading List

Allison, C. FitzSimons. *The Rise of Moralism: The Proclamation of the Gospel from Hooker to Baxter.* London, 1966.

———. *Stewardship of the Gospel.* Cincinnati, 1976.

Atkinson, James. *The Great Light: Luther and the Reformation.* Grand Rapids, 1968.

Avis, Paul. *Anglicanism and the Christian Churches: Theological Resources in Historical Perspective.* Minneapolis, 1989.

Aylmer, G. E., ed. *The Interregnum: The Quest for Settlement 1646-1660.* London, 1987.

Balleine, G. R. *A History of the Evangelical Party in the Church of England.* London, 1909.

Booty, John, and Stephen Sykes, eds. *The Study of Anglicanism.* Minneapolis, 1995.

Bray, Gerald, ed. *Documents of the English Reformation.* Minneapolis, 1994.

Brittain, Vera. *In the Steps of John Bunyan: An Excursion into Puritan England.* London, 1946.

Buchanan, Colin. "The Role and Calling of an Evangelical Theological College in the 1980's." *Churchman* 94, no. 1, offprinted Nottingham, 1980.

Butler, Diana Hochstedt. *Standing Against the Whirlwind: Evangelical Episcopalians in Nineteenth-Century America.* Oxford, 1995.

Chapman, Hester W. *Lady Jane Grey.* London, 1962.

Chatfield, Mark. *Churches the Victorians Forgot.* Ashbourne, Derbyshire, 1979.

Chorley, E. Clowes. *Men and Movements in the American Episcopal Church.* New York, 1948.

Collinson, Patrick. *The Religion of Protestants: The Church in English Society 1559-1625.* The Ford Lectures 1979. Oxford, 1985.

———. "The Late Medieval Church and Its Reformation (1400-1600)." In *The Oxford Illustrated History of Christianity,* edited by John McManners. Oxford and New York, 1990.

Cunningham, J. V., ed. *The Renaissance in England.* New York, 1966.

D'Aubigné, Agrippa. *Les Tragiques.* Gallimard edition. Paris, 1968.

Dickens, A. G. *The English Reformation.* 2d ed. London, 1993.

Eliot, George. *Scenes of Clerical Life.* Edited by Thomas S. Noble. Oxford, 1988.

Gillett, David K. *Trust and Obey: Explorations in Evangelical Spirituality.* London, 1993.

Greville, Fulke. *Selected Writings.* Edited by Joan Rees. London, 1973.

Griffith-Thomas, W. H. *The Principles of Theology.* London, 1978.

Guelzo, Allen C. *For the Union of Evangelical Christendom: The Irony of the Reformed Episcopalians.* University Park, Pa., 1994.

Guizot, François. *The History of Civilization in Europe.* London, 1997.

von Harnack, Adolf. *What Is Christianity?* Philadelphia, 1986.

Hennell, Michael. *Sons of the Prophets: Evangelical Leaders of the Victorian Church.* London, 1979.

Hill, Christopher. *The Collected Essays of Christopher Hill.* Vol. 2: *Religion and Politics in Seventeenth Century England.* Amherst, 1986.

Holmes, David C. "The Decline and Revival of the Church in Virginia." In *Up from Independence: The Episcopal Church in Virginia.* Orange, Va., 1976, pp. 45-101.

The Homilies of the Church of England. Lewes, E. Sussex, 1986.

Hooker, Richard. "A Learned Discourse of Justification." In *The Laws of Ecclesiastical Polity I.* London, 1954, pp. 14-76.

Hopkins, Hugh Evan. *Charles Simeon of Cambridge.* Grand Rapids, 1977.

Huntley, Frank Livingston. *Bishop Joseph Hall, 1574-1656.* Cambridge, 1979.

Kennedy, James W. *The Unknown Worshipper: A History of the Church of the Ascension.* New York, 1964.

Kingsley, Charles. *Westward Ho!* New York, 1948.

Lake, Peter. *Moderate Puritans and the Elizabethan Church.* Cambridge, 1982.

Litton, E. A. *Introduction to Dogmatic Theology.* Edited by Philip E. Hughes. London, 1960.

Macaulay, Thomas Babington. *The History of England.* London, 1986.

MacCulloch, Diarmaid. *Building a Godly Realm: The Establishment of English Protestantism.* London, 1992.

―――. *Thomas Cranmer: A Life.* New Haven and London, 1996.

Manwaring, Randle. *From Controversy to Co-Existence: Evangelicals in the Church of England 1914-1980.* Cambridge, 1985.

Massey, Don W. *The Episcopal Churches in the Diocese of Virginia.* Keswick, Va., 1989.

Moule, H. C. G., T. W. Drury, and R. B. Girdalstone, *English Church Teaching on Faith, Life and Order.* London, 1914.

O'Day, Rosemary. *The Debate on the English Reformation.* London and New York, 1986.

Packard, Joseph. *Recollections of a Long Life.* Washington, D.C., 1902.

Parker, T. H. L., ed. *English Reformers.* Philadelphia, 1966.

Prall, Stuart E. *The Bloodless Revolution: England 1688.* Madison, 1985.

Pratt, John H., ed. *The Thought of the Evangelical Leaders.* Edinburgh and Carlisle, Pa., 1978.

Prestwich, Menna, ed. *International Calvinism 1541-1715.* Oxford, 1985.

Rupp, Gordon. *Six Makers of English Religion 1500-1700.* New York, 1957.

Ryle, John Charles. *Charges and Addresses.* Edinburgh and Carlisle, Pa., 1978.

―――. *Christian Leaders of the Eighteenth Century.* Edinburgh and Carlisle, Pa., 1978.

―――. *Five English Reformers.* Edinburgh and Carlisle, Pa., 1994.

―――. *Knots Untied: Being Plain Statements on Disputed Points in Religion from the Standpoint of an Evangelical Churchman.* Cambridge, 1977.

Samuel, D. N., ed. *The Evangelical Succession in the Church of England.* Cambridge, 1979.

Saward, Michael. *Evangelicals on the Move.* London and Oxford, 1987.

Scotland, Nigel. *The Life and Work of John Bird Sumner: Evangelical Archbishop.* Cleominster, 1995.

Shaw, Bernard. *Saint Joan.* London, 1946.

Simeon, Charles. *Let Wisdom Judge: University Addresses and Sermon Outlines.* Edited by Arthur Pollard. Chicago, 1959.

Smyth, Charles. *Simeon and Church Order: A Study of the Origins of the Evangelical Revival in Cambridge in the Eighteenth Century.* The Birkbeck Lectures for 1937-1938. Cambridge, 1940.

Toon, Peter. *Evangelical Theology 1833-1856: A Response to Tractarianism.* Atlanta, 1979.

Toon, Peter, and Michael Smout, *John Charles Ryle: Evangelical Bishop.* Sterling, Va., 1976.

Tyndale, William. *Select Works.* Lewes, E. Sussex, 1986.

Tyng, Stephen H. *Recollections of England.* London, 1847.

Wace, Henry. *Principles of the Reformation: Practical and Historical Questions.* London, 1910.

Welsby, Paul A. *George Abbot: The Unwanted Archbishop.* London, 1962.

White, William Hale. *The Autobiography of Mark Rutherford.* Oxford, 1990.

Woolverton, John F. *The Education of Phillips Brooks.* Urbana and Chicago, 1995.

Zabriskie, Alexander C., ed. *Anglican Evangelicalism.* Philadelphia, 1943.

Articles of Religion
(The Thirty-Nine Articles)

As established by the Bishops, the Clergy, and the Laity of the
Protestant Episcopal Church in the United States of America,
in Convention, on the twelfth day of September, in the Year
of our Lord, 1801.

I. Of Faith in the Holy Trinity.

There is but one living and true God, everlasting, without body, parts, or passions; of infinite power, wisdom, and goodness; the Maker, and Preserver of all things both visible and invisible. And in unity of this Godhead there be three Persons, of one substance, power, and eternity; the Father, the Son, and the Holy Ghost.

II. Of the Word or Son of God, which was made very Man.

The Son, which is the Word of the Father, begotten from everlasting of the Father, the very and eternal God, and of one substance with the Father, took Man's nature in the womb of the blessed Virgin, of her substance: so that two whole and perfect Natures, that is to say, the Godhead and Manhood, were joined together in one Person, never to be divided, whereof is one Christ, very God, and very Man; who truly suffered, was crucified, dead, and buried, to reconcile his Father to us, and to be a sacrifice, not only for original guilt, but also for actual sins of men.

III. Of the going down of Christ into Hell.

As Christ died for us, and was buried; so also is it to be believed, that he went down into Hell.

IV. Of the Resurrection of Christ.

Christ did truly rise again from death, and took again his body, with flesh, bones, and all things appertaining to the perfection of Man's nature; wherewith he ascended into Heaven, and there sitteth, until he return to judge all Men at the last day.

V. Of the Holy Ghost.

The Holy Ghost, proceeding from the Father and the Son, is of one substance, majesty, and glory, with the Father and the Son, very and eternal God.

VI. Of the Sufficiency of the Holy Scriptures for Salvation.

Holy Scripture containeth all things necessary to salvation: so that whatsoever is not read therein, nor may be proved thereby, is not to be required of any man, that it should be believed as an article of the Faith, or be thought requisite or necessary to salvation. In the name of the Holy Scripture we do understand those canonical Books of the Old and New Testament, of whose authority was never any doubt in the Church.

Of the Names and Number of the Canonical Books.

Genesis,	The First Book of Samuel,	The Book of Esther,
Exodus,	The Second Book of Samuel,	The Book of Job,
Leviticus,	The First Book of Kings,	The Psalms,
Numbers,	The Second Book of Kings,	The Proverbs,
Deuteronomy,	The First Book of Chronicles,	Ecclesiastes or Preacher,
Joshua,	The Second Book of Chronicles,	Cantica, or Songs of Solomon,
Judges,	The First Book of Esdras,	Four Prophets the greater,
Ruth,	The Second Book of Esdras,	Twelve Prophets the less.

And the other Books (as Hierome saith) the Church doth read for example of life and instruction of manners; but yet doth it not apply them to establish any doctrine; such are these following:

The Third Book of Esdras,	The rest of the Book of Esther,
The Fourth Book of Esdras,	The Book of Wisdom,
The Book of Tobias,	Jesus the Son of Sirach,
The Book of Judith,	Baruch the Prophet,
The Song of the Three Children,	The Prayer of Manasses,
The Story of Susanna,	The First Book of Maccabees,
Of Bel and the Dragon,	The Second Book of Maccabees.

All the Books of the New Testament, as they are commonly received, we do receive, and account them Canonical.

VII. Of the Old Testament.

The Old Testament is not contrary to the New: for both in the Old and New Testament everlasting life is offered to Mankind by Christ, who is the only Mediator between God and Man, being both God and Man. Wherefore they are not to be heard, which feign that the old Fathers did look only for transitory promises. Although the Law given from God by Moses, as touching Ceremonies and Rites, do not bind Christian men, nor the Civil precepts thereof ought of necessity to be received in any commonwealth; yet notwithstanding, no Christian man whatsoever is free from the obedience of the Commandments which are called Moral.

VIII. Of the Creeds.

The Nicene Creed, and that which is commonly called the Apostles' Creed, ought thoroughly to be received and believed: for they may be proved by most certain warrants of Holy Scripture.

The original Article given Royal assent in 1571 and reaffirmed in 1662, was entitled "Of the Three Creeds"; and began as follows, "The Three Creeds, Nicene Creed, Athanasius's Creed, and that which is commonly called the Apostles' Creed. . . ."

IX. Of Original
or Birth-Sin.

Original sin standeth not in the following of Adam, (as the Pelagians do vainly talk;) but it is the fault and corruption of the Nature of every man, that naturally is engendered of the offspring of Adam; whereby man is very far gone from original righteousness, and is of his own nature inclined to evil, so that the flesh lusteth always contrary to the Spirit; and therefore in every person born into this world, it deserveth God's wrath and damnation. And this infection of nature doth remain, yea in them that are regenerated; whereby the lust of the flesh, called in Greek, φρόνημα σαρκός, (which some do expound the wisdom, some sensuality, some the affection, some the desire, of the flesh), is not subject to the Law of God. And although there is no condemnation for them that believe and are baptized; yet the Apostle doth confess, that concupiscence and lust hath of itself the nature of sin.

X. Of Free-Will.

The condition of Man after the fall of Adam is such, that he cannot turn and prepare himself, by his own natural strength and good works, to faith, and calling upon God. Wherefore we have no power to do good works pleasant and acceptable to God, without the grace of God by Christ preventing us, that we may have a good will, and working with us, when we have that good will.

XI. Of the Justification of Man.

We are accounted righteous before God, only for the merit of our Lord and Saviour Jesus Christ by Faith, and not for our own works or deservings. Wherefore, that we are justified by Faith only, is a most wholesome Doctrine, and very full of comfort, as more largely is expressed in the Homily of Justification.

XII. Of Good Works.

Albeit that Good Works, which are the fruits of Faith, and follow after Justification, cannot put away our sins, and endure the severity of God's judgment; yet are they pleasing and acceptable to God in Christ, and do spring out necessarily of a true and lively Faith; insomuch that by them a lively Faith may be as evidently known as a tree discerned by the fruit.

XIII. Of Works before Justification

Works done before the grace of Christ, and the Inspiration of his Spirit, are not pleasant to God, forasmuch as they spring not of faith in Jesus Christ; neither do they make men meet to receive grace, or (as the School-authors say) deserve grace of congruity: yea rather, for that they are not done as God hath willed and commanded them to be done, we doubt not but they have the nature of sin.

XIV. Of Works of Supererogation.

Voluntary Works besides, over and above, God's Commandments, which they call Works of Supererogation, cannot be taught without arrogancy and impiety: for by them men do declare, that they do not only render unto God as much as they are bound to do, but that they do more for his sake, than of bounden duty is required: whereas Christ saith plainly, When ye have done all that are commanded to you, say, We are unprofitable servants.

XV. Of Christ alone without Sin.

Christ in the truth of our nature was made like unto us in all things, sin only except, from which he was clearly void, both in his flesh, and in his spirit. He came to be the Lamb without spot, who, by sacrifice of himself once made, should take away the sins of the world; and sin (as Saint John saith) was not in him. But all we the rest, although baptized, and born again in Christ, yet offend in many things; and if we say we have no sin, we deceive ourselves, and the truth is not in us.

XVI. Of Sin after Baptism.

Not every deadly sin willingly committed after Baptism is sin against the Holy Ghost, and unpardonable. Wherefore the grant of repentance is not to be denied to such as fall into sin after Baptism. After we have received the Holy Ghost, we may depart from grace given, and fall into sin, and by the grace of God we may arise again, and amend our lives. And therefore they are to be condemned, which say, they can no more sin as long as they live here, or deny the place of forgiveness to such as truly repent.

XVII. Of Predestination and Election.

Predestination to Life is the everlasting purpose of God, whereby (before the foundations of the world were laid) he hath constantly decreed by his counsel secret to us, to deliver from curse and damnation those whom he hath chosen in Christ out of mankind, and to bring them by Christ to everlasting salvation, as vessels made to honour. Wherefore, they which be endued with so excellent a benefit of God, be called according to God's purpose by his Spirit working in due season: they through Grace obey the calling: they be justified freely: they be made sons of God by adoption: they be made like the image of his only-begotten Son Jesus Christ: they walk religiously in good works, and at length, by God's mercy, they attain to everlasting felicity.

As the godly consideration of Predestination, and our Election in Christ, is full of sweet, pleasant, and unspeakable comfort to godly persons, and such as feel in themselves the working of the Spirit of Christ, mortifying the works of the flesh, and their earthly members, and drawing up their mind to high and heavenly things, as well because it doth greatly establish and confirm their faith of eternal Salvation to be enjoyed through Christ, as because it doth fervently kindle their love towards God: So, for curious and carnal persons, lacking the Spirit of Christ, to have continually before their eyes the sentence of God's Predestination, is a most dangerous downfall, whereby the Devil doth thrust them either into desperation, or into wretchlessness of most unclean living, no less perilous than desperation.

Furthermore, we must receive God's promises in such wise, as they be generally set forth to us in Holy Scripture: and, in our doings, that Will of God is to be followed, which we have expressly declared unto us in the Word of God.

XVIII. Of obtaining eternal Salvation only by the Name of Christ.

They also are to be had accursed that presume to say, That every man shall be saved by the Law or Sect which he professeth, so that he be diligent to frame his life according to that Law, and the light of Nature. For Holy Scripture doth set out unto us only the Name of Jesus Christ, whereby men must be saved.

XIX. Of the Church.

The visible Church of Christ is a congregation of faithful men, in which the pure Word of God is preached, and the Sacraments be duly ministered according to Christ's ordinance, in all those things that of necessity are requisite to the same.

As the Church of Jerusalem, Alexandria, and Antioch, have erred; so also the Church of Rome hath erred, not only in their living and manner of Ceremonies, but also in matters of Faith.

XX. Of the Authority of the Church.

The Church hath power to decree Rites or Ceremonies, and authority in Controversies of Faith: and yet it is not lawful for the Church to ordain any thing that is contrary to God's Word written, neither may it so expound one place of Scripture, that it be repugnant to another. Wherefore, although the Church be a witness and a keeper of Holy Writ, yet, as it ought not to decree any thing against the same, so besides the same ought it not to enforce any thing to be believed for necessity of Salvation.

XXI. Of the Authority of General Councils.

[The Twenty-first of the former Articles is omitted; because it is partly of a local and civil nature, and is provided for, as to the remaining parts of it, in other Articles.]

The original 1571, 1662 text of this Article, omitted in the version of 1801, reads as follows: "General Councils may not be gathered together without the commandment and will of Princes. And when they be gathered together, (forasmuch as they be an assembly of men, whereof all be not governed with the Spirit and Word of God,) they may err, and sometimes have erred, even in things pertaining unto God. Wherefore things ordained by them as necessary to salvation have neither strength nor authority, unless it may be declared that they be taken out of holy Scripture."

XXII. Of Purgatory.

The Romish Doctrine concerning Purgatory, Pardons, Worshipping and Adoration, as well of Images as of Relics, and also Invocation of Saints, is a fond thing, vainly invented, and grounded upon no warranty of Scripture, but rather repugnant to the Word of God.

XXIII. Of Ministering in the Congregation.

It is not lawful for any man to take upon him the office of public preaching, or ministering the Sacraments in the Congregation, before he be lawfully called, and sent to execute the same. And those we ought to judge lawfully called and sent, which be chosen and called to this work by men who have public authority given unto them in the Congregation, to call and send Ministers into the Lord's vineyard.

XXIV. Of Speaking in the Congregation in such a Tongue as the people understandeth.

It is a thing plainly repugnant to the Word of God, and the custom of the Primitive Church, to have public Prayer in the Church, or to minister the Sacraments, in a tongue not understood of the people.

101

XXV. Of the Sacraments.

Sacraments ordained of Christ be not only badges or tokens of Christian men's profession, but rather they be certain sure witnesses, and effectual signs of grace, and God's good will towards us, by the which he doth work invisibly in us, and doth not only quicken, but also strengthen and confirm our Faith in him.

There are two Sacraments ordained of Christ our Lord in the Gospel, that is to say, Baptism, and the Supper of the Lord.

Those five commonly called Sacraments, that is to say, Confirmation, Penance, Orders, Matrimony, and Extreme Unction, are not to be counted for Sacraments of the Gospel, being such as have grown partly of the corrupt following of the Apostles, partly are states of life allowed in the Scriptures; but yet have not like nature of Sacraments with Baptism, and the Lord's Supper, for that they have not any visible sign or ceremony ordained of God.

The Sacraments were not ordained of Christ to be gazed upon, or to be carried about, but that we should duly use them. And in such only as worthily receive the same, they have a wholesome effect or operation: but they that receive them unworthily, purchase to themselves damnation, as Saint Paul saith.

XXVI. Of the Unworthiness of the Ministers, which hinders not the effect of the Sacraments.

Although in the visible Church the evil be ever mingled with the good, and sometimes the evil have chief authority in the Ministration of the Word and Sacraments, yet forasmuch as they do not the same in their own name, but in Christ's, and do minister by his commission and authority, we may use their Ministry, both in hearing the Word of God, and in receiving the Sacraments. Neither is the effect of Christ's ordinance taken away by their wickedness, nor the grace of God's gifts diminished from such as by faith, and rightly, do receive the Sacraments ministered unto them; which be effectual, because of Christ's institution and promise, although they be ministered by evil men.

Nevertheless, it appertaineth to the discipline of the Church, that inquiry be made of evil Ministers, and that they be accused by those that have knowledge of their offences; and finally, being found guilty, by just judgment be deposed.

XXVII. Of Baptism.

Baptism is not only a sign of profession, and mark of difference, whereby Christian men are discerned from others that be not christened, but it is also a sign of Regeneration or New-Birth, whereby, as by an instrument, they that receive Baptism rightly are grafted into the Church; the promises of the forgiveness of sin, and of our adoption to be the sons of God by the Holy Ghost, are visibly signed and sealed; Faith is confirmed, and Grace increased by virtue of prayer unto God.

The Baptism of young Children is in any wise to be retained in the Church, as most agreeable with the institution of Christ.

XXVIII. Of the Lord's Supper.

The Supper of the Lord is not only a sign of the love that Christians ought to have among themselves one to another; but rather it is a Sacrament of our Redemption by Christ's death: insomuch that to such as rightly, worthily, and with faith, receive the same, the Bread which we break is a partaking of the Body of Christ; and likewise the Cup of Blessing is a partaking of the Blood of Christ.

Transubstantiation (or the change of the substance of Bread and Wine) in the Supper of the Lord, cannot be proved by Holy Writ; but is repugnant to the plain words of Scripture, overthroweth the nature of a Sacrament, and hath given occasion to many superstitions.

The Body of Christ is given, taken, and eaten, in the Supper, only after an heavenly and spiritual manner. And the mean whereby the Body of Christ is received and eaten in the Supper, is Faith.

The Sacrament of the Lord's Supper was not by Christ's ordinance reserved, carried about, lifted up, or worshipped.

XXIX. Of the Wicked, which eat not the Body of Christ in the use of the Lord's Supper.

The Wicked, and such as be void of a lively faith, although they do carnally and visibly press with their teeth (as Saint Augustine saith) the Sacrament of the Body and Blood of Christ; yet in no wise are they partakers of Christ: but rather, to their condemnation, do eat and drink the sign or Sacrament of so great a thing.

XXX. Of both Kinds.

The Cup of the Lord is not to be denied to the Lay-people: for both the parts of the Lord's Sacrament, by Christ's ordinance and commandment, ought to be ministered to all Christian men alike.

XXXI. Of the one Oblation of Christ finished upon the Cross.

The Offering of Christ once made is that perfect redemption, propitiation, and satisfaction, for all the sins of the whole world, both original and actual; and there is none other satisfaction for sin, but that alone. Wherefore the sacrifices of Masses, in the which it was commonly said, that the Priest did offer Christ for the quick and the dead, to have remission of pain or guilt, were blasphemous fables, and dangerous deceits.

XXXII. Of the Marriage of Priests.

Bishops, Priests, and Deacons, are not commanded by God's Law, either to vow the estate of single life, or to abstain from marriage:

therefore it is lawful for them, as for all other Christian men, to marry at their own discretion, as they shall judge the same to serve better to godliness.

XXXIII. Of excommunicate Persons, how they are to be avoided.

That person which by open denunciation of the Church is rightly cut off from the unity of the Church, and excommunicated, ought to be taken of the whole multitude of the faithful, as an Heathen and Publican, until he be openly reconciled by penance, and received into the Church by a Judge that hath authority thereunto.

XXXIV. Of the Traditions of the Church.

It is not necessary that Traditions and Ceremonies be in all places one, or utterly like; for at all times they have been divers, and may be changed according to the diversity of countries, times, and men's manners, so that nothing be ordained against God's Word. Whosoever, through his private judgment, willingly and purposely, doth openly break the Traditions and Ceremonies of the Church, which be not repugnant to the Word of God, and be ordained and approved by common authority, ought to be rebuked openly, (that others may fear to do the like,) as he that offendeth against the common order of the Church, and hurteth the authority of the Magistrate, and woundeth the consciences of the weak brethren.

Every particular or national Church hath authority to ordain, change, and abolish, Ceremonies or Rites of the Church ordained only by man's authority, so that all things be done to edifying.

XXXV. Of the Homilies.

The Second Book of Homilies, the several titles whereof we have joined under this Article, doth contain a godly and wholesome Doctrine, and necessary for these times, as doth the former Book of Homilies, which were set forth in the time of Edward the Sixth; and therefore we judge them to be read in Churches by the Ministers, diligently and distinctly, that they may be understanded of the people.

Of the Names of the Homilies.

1. Of the right Use of the Church.
2. Against Peril of Idolatry.
3. Of repairing and keeping clean of Churches.
4. Of good Works: first of Fasting.
5. Against Gluttony and Drunkenness.
6. Against Excess of Apparel.
7. Of Prayer.
8. Of the Place and Time of Prayer.
9. That Common Prayers and Sacraments ought to be ministered in a known tongue.
10. Of the reverend Estimation of God's Word.
11. Of Alms-doing.
12. Of the Nativity of Christ.
13. Of the Passion of Christ.
14. Of the Resurrection of Christ.
15. Of the worthy receiving of the Sacrament of the Body and Blood of Christ.
16. Of the Gifts of the Holy Ghost.
17. For the Rogation-days.
18. Of the State of Matrimony.
19. Of Repentance.
20. Against Idleness.
21. Against Rebellion.

[This Article is received in this Church, so far as it declares the Books of Homilies to be an explication of Christian doctrine, and instructive in piety and morals. But all references to the constitution and laws of England are considered as inapplicable to the circumstances of this Church; which also suspends the order for the reading of said Homilies in churches, until a revision of them may be conveniently made, for the clearing of them, as well from obsolete words and phrases, as from the local references.]

XXXVI. Of Consecration of Bishops and Ministers.

The Book of Consecration of Bishops, and Ordering of Priests and Deacons, as set forth by the General Convention of this Church in

1792, doth contain all things necessary to such Consecration and Ordering; neither hath it any thing that, of itself, is superstitious and ungodly. And, therefore, whosoever are consecrated or ordered according to said Form, we decree all such to be rightly, orderly, and lawfully consecrated and ordered.

The original 1571, 1662 text of this Article reads as follows: "The Book of Consecration of Archbishops and Bishops, and Ordering of Priests and Deacons, lately set forth in the time of Edward the Sixth, and confirmed at the same time by authority of Parliament, doth contain all things necessary to such Consecration and Ordering: neither hath it any thing, that of itself is superstitious and ungodly. And therefore whosoever are consecrated or ordered according to the Rites of that Book, since the second year of the forenamed King Edward unto this time, or hereafter shall be consecrated or ordered according to the same Rites; we decree all such to be rightly, orderly, and lawfully consecrated and ordered."

XXXVII. Of the Power of the Civil Magistrates.

The Power of the Civil Magistrate extendeth to all men, as well Clergy as Laity, in all things temporal; but hath no authority in things purely spiritual. And we hold it to be the duty of all men who are professors of the Gospel, to pay respectful obedience to the Civil Authority, regularly and legitimately constituted.

The original 1571, 1662 text of this Article reads as follows: "The King's Majesty hath the chief power in this Realm of England, and other his Dominions, unto whom the chief Government of all Estates of this Realm, whether they be Ecclesiastical or Civil, in all causes doth appertain, and is not, nor ought to be, subject to any foreign Jurisdiction. Where we attribute to the King's Majesty the chief government, by which Titles we understand the minds of some slanderous folks to be offended; we give not our Princes the ministering either of God's Word, or of the Sacraments, the which thing the Injunctions also lately set forth by Elizabeth our Queen do most plainly testify; but that only prerogative, which we see to have been given always to all godly Princes in holy Scriptures by God himself; that is, that they should rule all estates and degrees committed to their charge by God, whether they be Ecclesiastical or Temporal, and restrain with the civil sword the stubborn and evil-doers.

The Bishop of Rome hath no jurisdiction in this Realm of England.

The Laws of the Realm may punish Christian men with death, for heinous and grievous offences.

It is lawful for Christian men, at the commandment of the Magistrate, to wear weapons, and serve in the wars."

XXXVIII. Of Christian Men's Goods, which are not common.

The Riches and Goods of Christians are not common, as touching the right, title, and possession of the same; as certain Anabaptists do falsely boast. Notwithstanding, every man ought, of such things as he possesseth, liberally to give alms to the poor, according to his ability.

XXXIX. Of a Christian Man's Oath.

As we confess that vain and rash Swearing is forbidden Christian men by our Lord Jesus Christ, and James his Apostle, so we judge, that Christian Religion doth not prohibit, but that a man may swear when the Magistrate requireth, in a cause of faith and charity, so it be done according to the Prophet's teaching in justice, judgment, and truth.

APPENDIX B

The Risky Question

(A Sermon Preached August 24, 1997, at Canterbury Cathedral)

Today is St. Bartholomew's Day. My mind turns to the tragic events of St. Bartholomew's Day 1572, events which the great American filmmaker D. W. Griffith likened to the Passion of Christ in his masterpiece *Intolerance*. St. Bartholomew's Day 1572 was the day on which thousands were martyred for their faith, in France. Cardinal Odet de Coligny, who had departed the Church of Rome and whose brother was murdered that night in Paris, got out in time. He is buried here in Canterbury Cathedral in the Trinity Chapel.

The distant memory of that "crime of the century," depicted accurately and movingly in the current London musical *Martin Guerre*, gives us a point from which to think again about the heart of the matter. What gave those "protesting" Christians the courage and serenity to bear bitter persecution for conscience' sake? It must have been close to the bone. What would be sufficient to endow any one of us with the confidence to believe that "Christian" is the one name worth bearing above all names, no matter what the cost to ourselves? What is the heart of the matter?

The heart of the matter, the very center of Christianity, is the answer to *one risky question*. There are many questions we can ask in relation to God: What is the origin of suffering, particularly innocent suffering? Why do some people believe in God, and others not? Where do we come from, who are we, and where are we going? (That is the title of a mural painting by Paul Gauguin which hangs in the Boston Museum of Fine Arts.) These first questions we might call *"risk-free" questions*. They are risk-free questions because they are abstract. They are questions which are "out there." They may conceal or veil a more personal question, such as, Why am *I* suffering? Or why has God allowed this to happen to *me?* But in themselves they are primarily intellectual questions. They are subjects for the debating society, the never-ending college bull session.

The most commonly posed example of a risk-free question is this: Why do the guilty prosper and the innocent suffer? Not only is this question an intellectual one, usually framed in terms of groups and categories of persons; but it is also unanswerable. There is no answer to this question, even in Scripture. The ultimate cause of the continuing existence of unfairness in the world is not knowable — at least it never has been known, or understood, in such a way that most people are convinced.

Most questions commonly asked about God are *risk-free questions*. That is, even the answers, if we knew them, would not necessarily affect you and me directly. Risk-free questions are abstract questions.

But there is *one risky question*. It is this question: How can I be *justified? This* question has been put by persons as diverse as St. Augustine of Hippo in the fourth century, Thomas Cranmer in the sixteenth century, and, within a wholly different universe, Sam Pekinpah, the film director, in our own time. Pekinpah, by the way, said that the single question he pondered day and night his entire life was, How can I go down to my house justified? We can paraphrase the question in a more contemporary way: How can my personal existence amount to anything that endures? How can I be legitimized? How can I be recognized, evaluated, *valued*, in such a way that my life will add up to something?

To put it negatively, what prevents my life from being judged a failure? What is able to defend my life from the charge of mismanagement, mis-use, *a*-buse, "the things done and the things left undone"?

What will prevent me, on the basis of the life I have lived, from being found *wanting*, from being regarded as a failure in comparison to someone else, from being left out and judged unworthy of praise?

The *one risky question* of our justification can thus be put in two ways: How can I *find* justification? or How can I *defeat* accusation? These two questions are the same question. And if you know anything of the wincing pain of being accused of something, whether truly or falsely, you will agree that this is not a risk-free question. It is a *risky* question. How can I be justified?

Is this clear? — the distinction between risk-free questions in religion and *the risky question?* The risky question is the important one. (You can now therefore resign from the debating society!) This is the question of our lives: How can we be accounted righteous, or worthy of acceptance, by the other?

The New Testament states that the great step of God's Incarnation took place for a purpose. "The Word became flesh and dwelt among us" (St. John 1:14) for a purpose. The end to which Christ came among us became apparent as a result of his death and resurrection. This is put to us succinctly in the twenty-fifth verse of the fourth chapter of Romans, where St. Paul writes, "Our Lord Jesus was raised for our justification." The purpose for which he came down to us was *to justify us*, us who are asking ourselves consciously or unconsciously the gnawing question, How can I be justified?

This question of justification is the root cause of what we today call *stress*. Stress is the experience of having to do (or believing one has to do) more things than one thinks one possibly *can* do, and having to do them perfectly, or ideally, or however you want to say it — just right! When you feel *stress*, you are asking yourself, How can I be justified? and you are answering the question for yourself *in the negative*. I can't be!

This came home to me personally in a conversation exactly twenty years ago. I had just submitted a manuscript for a book to a publisher in New York City. I was telling a friend about it who was a professional art historian. She asked me, "How do you feel about the manuscript?" I replied, "Well, I guess I *think* it's pretty good." She commented, "Great. If *you* think it's good, that's all that matters." "Yuh," I said compliantly. But what I really *thought* was: "NO, it *doesn't* matter what *I* think, at all! The only thing that matters is what the publisher thinks. The only thing that matters is what *they* think!!"

My inward being was fixed on the question, How can I be justified? And I could not do this for myself, as my nonneurotic friend had implied I could. I needed to be justified, to be given the passing grade, by the *other*. This is the great and pressing issue of biblical religion.

St. Paul in Romans, chapter four, wants us to hear that *we have been justified.* "Christ was put to death for our trespasses," as the first part of verse 25 says, "and he was raised for our justification." Our sins having been forgiven, the burden of our past having been put away, we can rise with Christ — justified — looking forward to an unshadowed future.

What this means is that *the* question of our lives — how can I be justified (or, in present parlance, esteemed, accepted, *included*)? — has been answered decisively. It has been answered by a true miracle, the resurrection of Jesus, the book-end to Christmas, unprecedented, unique, and complete, entirely outside our best (insufficient) efforts to justify *ourselves*. It is not only the forgiveness of sins by means of the atoning death of Christ. That was a negation of the negative. It was, and is also, the justification of our present shaky lives by the rising of Christ to unending life. It is an affirmation of the positive. Easter has confirmed the forgiving effect of Good Friday such that it is valid everlastingly.

Will you receive this?

"Therefore, since we are justified by faith, we have peace with God through our Lord Jesus Christ. Through him we have obtained access to this grace in which we stand, and we rejoice in our hope of sharing the glory of God" (Rom. 5:1-2).

In the words of Archbishop Cranmer, let us pray:

Almighty Father, who hast given thine only Son to die for our sins, and to rise again for our justification; Grant us so to put away the leaven of malice and wickedness, that we may always serve thee in pureness of living and truth; through the merits of the same thy Son Jesus Christ our Lord. Amen.

112